KOOTENAY COUNTRY

ONE MAN'S LIFE IN THE
CANADIAN ROCKIES

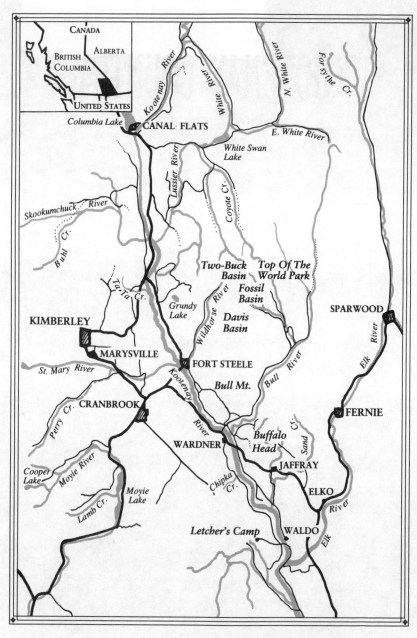

SOUTHERN SECTION, EAST KOOTENAY REGION, BRITISH COLUMBIA
(SEE INSET FOR LOCATION)

KOOTENAY COUNTRY

ONE MAN'S LIFE IN THE
CANADIAN ROCKIES

ERNEST F. "FEE" HELLMEN

With a Foreword by Andy Russell

Alaska Northwest Books™
Anchorage • Seattle

DEDICATION

In memory of
Bayard O. Iverson,
who taught me to read and write.

Library of Congress Cataloging-in-Publication Data
Hellmen, Ernest F., 1918-
Kootenay Country : one man's life in the Canadian Rockies /
by Ernest F. "Fee" Hellmen.
p. cm.
ISBN 0-88240-357-5
1. Kootenai River Valley—Social life and customs.
2. Hellmen, Ernest F., 1918-   . 3. Kootenai River
Valley—Biography. 4. Outdoor life—Kootenai River Valley. I. Title.
F1089.K7H44   1990
971.1'6504'092—dc20
[B]   89-17893   CIP

Photographs are courtesy of Fee Hellmen, except: page 130, courtesy of the
British Columbia Archives and Records Services, Victoria (cat. no. 83591);
page 131 (FS 21.11) and back cover (FS 21.14), courtesy of the Archives, Fort
Steele Heritage Park, Fort Steele, British Columbia.

Edited by Ethel Dassow and Ellen Harkins Wheat
Design by Alyson Hallberg
Cover design by Kate Thompson

Alaska Northwest Books™
22026 20th Avenue S.E.
Bothell, Washington 98021
A division of GTE Discovery Publications, Inc.

Printed in U.S.A.

CONTENTS

III THE HUNT

IV GUIDING ON THE MOYIE

V REFLECTIONS

FOREWORD

THERE ARE VERY FEW OF US left in this world of jet travel, computers and modern homes who know what it is to grow up, raise a family and live in real wilderness country, where staying alive depends on hunting skill, picking fruit off bushes, growing vegetables in a garden and knowing how to be comfortable in an Indian tipi.

Ernest F. "Fee" Hellmen knows exactly how it feels. He has written his book, KOOTENAY COUNTRY, in the style of a good campfire raconteur to record his life as a hunter, naturalist, professional guide and outfitter in the beautiful East Kootenay country of British Columbia, Canada. This vast area of mountains, lakes and wild rivers was, until a few years ago, a part of the world that was home to one of the greatest wildlife populations to be found anywhere on the globe.

In an easygoing, informative and humorous way he tells how it was to live as a hunter and gatherer, the primitive kind of living off the land at a time when radios were scarce, television had yet to be thought of and wheels were something to be used only when you came down into the bottoms of the valleys. The East Kootenay is mountain country as rugged and wild as the Rockies can get; the peaks cleave the sky like spires of nature's cathedrals. Some men used horses to get up into the high timberline basins, but others, like Fee, lashed their camps on packboards slung over their shoulders and walked to places where horses could never get — lovely, remote canyons and meadows where little streams sang among the rocks and wind and storms played the music of the peaks so familiar to the ears of mountain men. They stepped into adventure almost every day, in a terrain where the careful placing of a climbing boot can mean the difference between life and death.

Fee Hellmen is a master storyteller, who practiced the art around uncounted campfires while the smoke rose and lost itself among a million stars. Luckily for us, he went further and put his stories in writing, to share with us what he has seen of those grand times when the big timber was untouched and the mountain streams were pristine — as clear and cold and pure as glacier ice. His book is a living monument to majestic country and good times gone by.

—Andy Russell
Alberta, Canada

PREFACE

ERNEST FRIDOLF HELLMEN (that's me) was born at Wardner, British Columbia, on March 9, 1918. My sister, Teresia, was then ten years old. Many years later she told me of the difficulties Mother and I shared through that long and painful night.

My birth took place in a two-room log cabin across the Kootenay River from town. Two midwives were in attendance, and they had brought a bottle of dark rum in preparation for a long vigil. As the labor dragged on the level of rum in the bottle lowered until, shortly before dawn, both ladies were pretty well inebriated and Mother, with a minimum of help, produced a ten-pound son. Considering that she was forty, already had three children, and her last delivery had been eight years earlier, that was no mean feat.

Looming large to the north of my place of birth was the huge, dark mass of Bull Mountain. As I became aware of the world around me, this majestic phenomenon, along with the jagged and beautiful Rocky Mountain Range to the east, attracted my attention and, probably because of their dominance in a wee boy's first awareness, set the stage for a lifetime love affair.

Nearer at hand, still mostly covered with virgin timber, was the lower range of the Pickering Hills. My father worked hard in the logging camps there, busily denuding the slopes and gullies with saw and ax. Often, on the day of the week when he was not working, he went back with rifle and knife, hunting the deer that inhabited the thickets. This he did not only for the thrill of the hunt but also to contribute to the larder.

My father had a great respect and love for wild things, large and small. No doubt it was he who showed me the first animal I saw, perhaps a chipmunk in our woodpile, or a raven sitting on a snag. In any case, I soon became aware of the natural denizens in our little part of the world. When I consider these things now I realize that, although the hills and mountains are things of mystery and beauty, without the wildlife to animate them they would not be so interesting and appealing.

Naturally when Father was home he spoke of his work. The camps where he stayed during the week were designated by number and name: Camp Seven, Camp Nine, Camp Seventeen, Weatherhead's Slough, Jule's Landing — places where all sorts of exciting things happened. To Father they were everyday occurrences, part of the job, but to a little boy they were high adventure, and from the time I was first able to comprehend, I longed to visit those fabulous places. I visited the nearer ones first with my older brothers, but as I grew older and more confident I extended my perambulations alone. By twelve or so I was fairly well acquainted with the whole area from the Kootenay River to the foot of the Rockies.

The Kootenay River, which flows through a great valley, was another source of fascination. I spent many dangerous hours playing along the banks of that turbulent stream, and it is a wonder I didn't drown in the cold waters.

I killed my first deer up on Pickering Hill. I was still a boy, but I remember vividly how my companion ran the deer in front of me. A little yearling doe, she stopped momentarily to scan her back-trail, and I fired the fatal shot. She was the first of many — too many, perhaps. But that was in the thirties, survival was the name of the game, and we heeded not the game regulations. Neither did we shoot for pleasure. While we ignored the official regulations, we had rules of our own to which we adhered strictly: we were never to kill more than we needed for our immediate wants; we were to avoid at all costs wounding and losing game that would linger in pain; and we were not to kill game unless the species was abundant.

This was the tradition in which I grew up. It was a life concerned mainly with hunting, fishing, the Great Outdoors and the wildlife that inhabits it. My stories are not unusual. They are the remembrances of an average person of the period. But they are recollections of a time and place that is special to me. Some of these stories stand out in my memory, and I have set them down in this book.

AUTHOR'S NOTE OF THANKS

I would like to thank my good friends Don Edlund
and Derryll White for their invaluable help
in the writing of this book.
Also, Struan Robertson gave his unstinting support
to me during a very difficult phase of my life
coinciding with the writing.

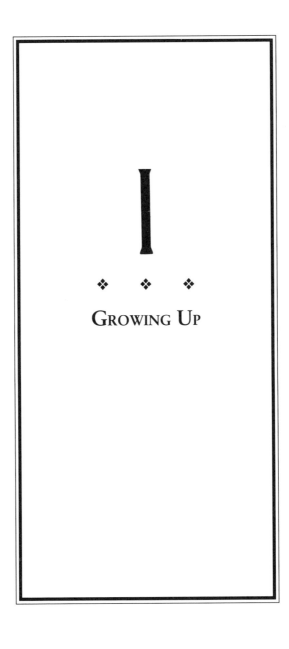

I

❖   ❖   ❖

GROWING UP

Boys Along the Kootenay

❖   ❖   ❖

FROM TIME TO TIME ON A lazy evening I rise from my chair, turn the TV off and the light down to low beam, sit back down and relax, and close my eyes. . . .

❖   ❖   ❖

It's the last half of April, 1927. Saturday. Two nine-year-old boys are walking across the Kootenay River bridge at Wardner. Each of them carries an old tubular steel fishing pole, taken down into sections for easy carrying, and tied with bits of string to prevent loss of one of the parts.

Jutting from the back pockets of their knickers are the handles of slingshots, in their right-hand pockets a supply of rocks — each one carefully chosen for weight and shape.

Both youngsters are Canadian-born, the dark-haired one of Japanese parents, the blond of Swedish descent. They are friends, real buddies.

They reach the center of the bridge where the current below them is the strongest, and leaning dangerously far out over the railing, they spit in the river. That's for luck. Everyone knows you won't have any luck fishing unless you spit in the river first.

Just across the river is Sjoholm's farm. A number of gophers sit upright on their home mounds, but all are too far away for any but the luckiest shot. The boys raise their slingshots and fire in unison at the nearest, which promptly bolts down its burrow, unharmed.

They walk on across the river flat, flipping rocks at various targets. The road is dead straight here for half a mile, bordered on both sides with dense thickets of red willow. Spotted here and there among the willows are clumps of mature spruce, towering dark green against the cobalt sky.

They nearly reach the slough, a dark, stagnant channel of the river, when they hear a car approaching from behind. While cars are not yet common, the boys recognize this one as an old cloth-topped touring car, red with rust, not worthy of attention. As it passes they see that the side curtains are up, and they make out several indistinct shapes through the clouded celluloid.

The road here is damp with capillary action from the water table below. There is no dust. The rear of the car has two gaping holes where the small oval rear windows have been broken out. Idly the blond boy flips a rock after the moving car. To his dismay he sees the rock disappear through one of the holes.

The car grinds to a shuddering halt. The blond boy walks toward it, intending to apologize for the unfortunate incident. A man steps from the car. Heavens to Betsy! From braids to moccasins he is one huge Indian warrior!

Custer's Last Stand is not that far in the past, and there are many stories of Indian raids still making the rounds. Besides, both boys have been reading James Fenimore Cooper. With one accord they scramble through the roadside ditch and seek cover in the willows. After they have run for some distance they pause to regain their breath, and turn toward each other, laughing.

They hear a crashing amongst the willows not far behind them. A sudden, awful truth dawns: it is the Indian in pursuit! If they can hear him, he can hear them. There will be no escape! Really frightened now, they dash desperately on, fighting the clutching willows.

They come to a wide cattle trail weaving through the brush. They turn left along it, taking care not to step in the telltale dust, running on the grassy border.

Suddenly they are confronted by the slough. Too late they discover they have turned the wrong way on the trail and are now cornered. The slough is too deep to wade across, and although they would not admit it, neither one can swim. They have often wondered what it would feel like to be scalped, and now it would seem they have a good chance of finding out. They crawl deep into a thicket and huddle there, waiting to feel the awful pain of the knife.

After an interminable time they hear the old car start up and rattle off over the washboard road toward Jaffray, and they have the distinct impression that they heard loud laughter. Could it be that the Indian was funning them?

Cautiously they return to the road, mindful all the while of a possible ambush. The car is gone, and apparently the Indian too.

They cross the slough on the bridge and walk on across the flat to the big gravel pit at the foot of the Bull River Hill. Here they replenish their supply of rocks, then climb the hill to the Canadian Pacific railroad track. They follow the track northward up the Kootenay toward Bull River, stepping on the ties with every other footstep and seeing how far they can walk the rails without falling off.

They find a turtle trapped between the rails, and after inspecting him closely and scratching their trademark, "F & C Co.," on his shell, turn him loose on the river side of the track. Everyone knows a turtle has to have water.

A short time later they turn savage and kill a hapless chipmunk with their slingshots.

Cutting down to the river from the track, in a back-eddy they find a boat someone has recently tarred. Stuck in the soft tar is an insect neither of them has seen before. Fascinated, they watch it writhing and twisting as it seeks to free itself. Then, to their utter astonishment, they realize they are watching the metamorphosis of a dragonfly from nymph to adult, just as Mr. Iverson, their teacher, had described in Nature Study.

First the skin of the nymph begins to split, then slowly and with much effort the adult dragonfly emerges, perfectly formed with wings folded. Daintily it stands on its shed case, avoiding the sticky tar, and they watch with faces pressed closed while its wings dry and unfold. After a long time the insect flies off, gossamer wings twinkling in the sun. The boys make a game of which one can see the farthest. Both of them lie a little bit.

Then on up the river to the big backwater just below the mouth of the Bull River. Here the combined waters swirl and roll with awesome power. When the boys stand still and listen closely they hear a sound like rustling silk, and they believe the sound is made by two rivers rubbing together.

They like the muddy smell of the river. When they kneel to drink, the water tastes muddy too, but it is faint and not unpleasant. For a long time they fish the eddy, each one getting a cutthroat trout of about a pound, the dark-haired boy catching a char a little bigger. Eager cries — "I got one on!" "I had a bite!" "Aw, I got a snag!" — fly back and forth.

The lowering sun gives warning that it is time to go. Both boys are famished. The long walk home is a series of small adventures, but finally it is time to part at the blond one's door.

"What'll we do tomorrow?"

"I dunno."

"Let's go down to the Chipka and work on the cave."

"Good idea. We'll get that big rock out of the hole. I'll swipe Pa's cold chisel and hammer."

"Good! See you in the morning!"

It's a long time since boys have sipped the waters of the Kootenay. The pulp mill at Skookumchuck took care of that. And the rustling waters, where they enter the Libby Dam impoundment called Lake Koocanusa, are stilled forever.

Running Logs

❖ ❖ ❖

THE HILLS AND MOUNTAINS of our glorious part of the world held enchantment, but the river . . . ah, the river! We boys spent much of our time along its banks, and many of our adventures were of the dangerous kind.

There was an island in the middle of the Kootenay River, and on the channel on the west side was the Crow's Nest Pass Lumber Company's big steam-powered sawmill. A row of pilings had been driven in this channel to contain the logs for the mill in what was called the pond. A floating boom, consisting of a double row of logs linked with short lengths of heavy chain and decked with planking, ran from the pilings across to the mill. The purpose of this boom was to direct the logs destined for the head-rig to the jack-ladder.

The mill-pond was kept nearly full of logs, and we boys were irresistibly drawn to play a game called "running logs." Nearly any summer evening after the mill was shut down for the day, a small party of us would be down there running across the floating logs. Almost invariably we would continue our game until one or another of us fell in. Usually this meant simply slipping off one of the wet logs, whereupon we would cling to it until we were able to pull ourselves back to safety, perhaps with the help of one of our friends. We would then dry our clothes so our parents wouldn't know what we'd been up to.

Few of us could swim, and there was always a distinct possibility that the current would carry us underneath a solid mass of logs, with very sad results. We were repeatedly warned that we must never, never play near the pond. This order was easily circumvented by saying we were going over to the schoolyard to play hide-and-go-seek. If some of our family happened to pass by and not see us with the rest of the group, they would naturally think we were hiding.

When we were out of sight of home, we would make a beeline for the pond. It was imperative that we return home in a dry state, however, or we would be in trouble. This we managed by sneaking into a boiler-room of the sawmill, where steam was produced twenty-four hours of the day. There were four huge steam boilers, heavily bricked in, and the topmost bricks were hot from the steam within. We would strip off our wet clothes, lay them on the hot bricks, and in fifteen minutes or so they were dry. A night fireman was in attendance, of course, but he turned a blind eye to our escapades. I think he had once been a boy himself.

Some of the older boys were so well practiced that they could cross over the floating logs from the bank on the mill side to the boom without falling in. It was a great challenge to us younger ones to duplicate this feat. Once we had mastered it, we joined the ranks above us, a step up the ladder of our hierarchy.

One memorable evening when the river was quite high and a stiff current was running (I shudder to remember it now), I decided to meet the challenge. There appeared to be a solid mass of logs from the mill to the boom, a distance of possibly two hundred feet. I struck off. The trick was to run lightly and swiftly over the smaller logs that would not support your weight, pausing when you came to a larger, stable log to chart a course to the next big one.

Unfortunately I came to a long run of small ones, and was forced to keep skipping along like a weightless cat. I was nearly to the boom when I ran out of logs. There was nothing in front of me but ten feet of open water. I had no alternative but to cast myself into the water in a desperate belly flop, in the forlorn hope of reaching the boom before going under. I didn't make it. The water closed over my head well short of the boom. The current rolled me over and carried me under. The water boiled up in the lee of the boom, and I was cast to the surface within arm's reach of the boom, but the smooth, round, wet surface of the boom log was impossible to grasp.

At irregular intervals along the boom, spikes were driven in for half their length for the purpose of mooring a raft that the workmen kept handy. One of these spikes was just within reach. I managed to crook one finger over it. The current had my body stretched right out, with nothing but miles of turbulent water downstream. It took all the effort I could muster to draw my body back to the boom.

Oddly enough, there was no sensation of fear. A week or so later I made the crossing without incident, and joined the rank of the Big Boys.

Anchors Aweigh

❖ ❖ ❖

As if the Kootenay didn't already hold enough enchantment for us, a character calling himself Mark Twain had to write a couple of books that really inflamed our imaginations.

If Huckleberry Finn and Tom Sawyer could do it, so could we. Granted, our brawling river was of a different character from the broad, placid Mississippi, but it was all we had. And so it transpired that one day in April three of us began constructing a raft. We were not very big, or strong, so our raft was built of what small, dry logs and poles we could move by hand from the bottom land near the railroad bridge to a convenient backwater. We tacked it together with nails and spikes we swiped from our fathers, taking care not to raise undue suspicion.

The finished product was not very handsome, and much too small for what we had in mind. When we launched her in the placid backwater below the bridge we found she wouldn't properly bear the weight of all three of us. She settled until the water lapped our boots. She wasn't very solid, either, and we could feel the logs shifting beneath our feet. It seemed that the whole thing would disintegrate at any moment.

That wasn't quite what we had expected, but we shoved off with a couple of short poles. We intended a brief shakedown cruise around the eddy, but before we knew it we were out of the depth of our poles. The current had grabbed us, and in a few scary moments we were careening grandly downstream. By dint of much effort, using our poles as paddles, we could keep fairly close to shore, and we traveled on at high speed in a high state of excitement.

We came around the first bend and found to our horror that the main bulk of the water pinched in to our side of the river. Below us on the reverse curve was a huge logjam against the bank, with the greater part of the water rushing underneath it. The force of the water hitting the jam threw a spray high onto the logs.

The river picked up speed and carried us directly to the jam. Ignorant though we were, we realized that our half-sunken craft would hit the jam and tip down on the upper side, whereupon the force of the water would carry it and us underneath the tangle of debris. Our survival would depend on leaping for the logs the instant our raft struck. Just as we were anticipating the collision we saw a hefty log projecting ten feet or so upstream, just under the surface. Our raft was going to hit it, and we would still be too far from the main jam to jump.

All three of us leaped and landed ankle deep on the slippery log. Clinging to each other for support, we somehow managed to keep our balance and walk to safety. Our raft was sucked into the black water under the jam, to be seen no more.

We had learned an important lesson: we needed a bigger raft and longer poles. It took us some time to collect the spikes we needed. We also managed to come by a goodly length of light rope with which we hoped to bind the logs together more firmly. One of our number, showing good sense for a change, declined to take another cruise, but did help with the construction of our new craft.

My remaining partner and I found ourselves on another day floating merrily downstream. It was May and the Kootenay was showing signs of coming into the flood stage, but not yet rolling along with the vicious power it would show a little later. Our raft this time was more substantial, although far from safe. With the knowledge we had gained in our first attempt, we poled across to the other side of the river to avoid the logjam where we had nearly come to grief on our first trip. We passed the jam in fine style and slipped down the river at an astonishing pace. We passed a couple of islands we would have liked to explore, but we felt we couldn't spare the time.

Just above the mouth of the Chipka Creek we rounded a bend and found ourselves facing another terrifying prospect. We were being sucked into a great rapid — real white water with wave crests that seemed to be three feet high. We thought our raft would be tossed around like a cork, perhaps capsized. But our sluggish craft ploughed through instead of pitching over the waves. It was a rough ride, but not nearly as bad as we had feared. As we passed through the crests we were knee-deep in water; in the troughs the raft ran on the surface. And we found that, since our speed was identical to that of the water, there was really no danger of being washed overboard. Nevertheless it was a thrilling two-hundred-yard ride, and we anticipated more of the same ahead. Alas! We were disappointed.

With the calmer waters we had the opportunity to relax and study the river and the many intriguing possibilities it revealed. High on the western bank, in the face of a cliff, we saw a cave that would bear investigating. We passed over deep green pools that we were sure must harbor some huge Dolly Varden trout. We were impressed by the many whirlpools and boils that appeared and disappeared with the changes in the current. There was much sign of beaver activity along the shore, and we thought we would come again with some traps and make our fortune in furs. The fresh spring foliage was at its brightest and best, the light breeze loaded with fragrance.

Down near Plumbob Creek we grounded our craft in a backwater, clambered to firm ground, and then faced the long journey home on foot.

The Slingshot

❖   ❖   ❖

I WAS FORTUNATE IN BEING the youngest of our family, so I had plenty of coaching when I finally graduated to handling my older brother's .22 rifle. But I think what helped me most was the experience in the use of the slingshot. I found it easy to understand such terms as trajectory, windage, lead, velocity, drop and ricochet. I had actually observed many thousands of projectiles in flight, and these observations were invaluable in understanding the broader term, ballistics. I also absorbed some fine lessons in safety while hunting small game with the slingshot.

My proper age for the slingshot happened to coincide with those days in the 1920s when the automobile first came into general use. Flat tires were nearly a daily occurrence, and there was any amount of good live rubber available from discarded inner tubes.

The slingshot was contrived by the Devil, I'm sure, with the intention of leading small boys directly to perdition. Being naturally bloodthirsty creatures, we boys seize avidly on this invention.

The river bottom where the red willow grew would provide the necessary crotch (or crutch) for the forepart of the weapon. This crutch was selected with great care to ensure that the limbs were absolutely symmetrical. It was permissible to select a crutch with one limb slightly larger than the other, since the larger limb could be dressed down by scraping it with a shard of broken glass to the exact dimensions of the other.

The limbs of the crutch were never straight. It was imperative that they be slightly curved, forming a delicate U. The crutches were never carved nor otherwise decorated, their beauty being in the sweeping simplicity of line. The boys of each village and town developed weapons distinctive in character. The boys from Bull River to the north and Jaffray to the south bore weapons much inferior to ours, not only in effectiveness but in aesthetic appeal as well.

Two strips of rubber cut from an old inner tube with Mother's best scissors ("Ow! Ma!") provided the power to drive the rock. (Never, never was it called a pebble.) A soft leather pouch cut from an old boot tongue or the back of a lumber mitt held the rock until it was released. Assembled to certain rigid specifications with bits of "store" string, the result was a weapon that should never have been entrusted to a boy.

Nevertheless, each of us owned one or more of these, and by incessant practice we grew extremely proficient in their use. There was no apparatus for aiming or sighting; shooting was instinctive. A rock was placed in the pouch, the rubber drawn, the whole contraption pointed toward the target, and the rock released. After thousands of shots the rocks began to find the mark, and some of us became almost uncanny in our accuracy.

Inevitably there sprang up an intense rivalry among us as to who was the best shot and could kill the most small game.

Some of the game wasn't so small, either. I once inadvertently killed our neighbor's black-and-white tomcat at extreme range. It happened one morning when I came out of our house on the way to school. The cat was stalking a bluebird near a pile of slabwood down the street. Thinking to scare off either the cat or the bird, I hauled back on the rubber and let fly. The rock arched nicely through the air and struck the cat right behind the ear.

I confessed what I had done to the neighbor boy and we cooked up a yarn about having seen the cat run over by a car. This, we thought, was better than losing our precious weapons. See what I mean when I refer to the Devil?

Anyway, the moral of that accident was not lost on me; never point a slingshot — or a gun — at anything you don't intend to shoot.

I had a great horned owl to my credit (credit?) and innumerable chipmunks, gophers and assorted birds. Some of the birds, I'm sorry to say, were songbirds, although we did try to make a distinction between, say, bluebirds on the one hand and English sparrows on the other. English sparrows at that time were the equivalent in numbers of the starlings today. Thousands of them nested in the lumber piles down by the big mill. Rabbits and grouse, too, fell to my slingshot, and often made a welcome addition to our table.

One summer evening when I was about ten years old I was hurrying home from a day in the hills. I came to a little slough with a nice big green-head mallard paddling on the surface. Of course I attempted a stalk, but that canny old drake watched my efforts with contempt. He waited a bit too long with his takeoff. The slough was in a deep pocket surrounded by hills, and he had to circle once for altitude before he could level off.

At what seemed his nearest point to me, I aimed considerably ahead of him and let a rock fly with all the power I could draw from the rubber. The rock seemed to travel in a long arc, and it homed in perfectly on the side of his head. He spiralled to earth just as dead as if he had been struck by a charge from a twelve-gauge shotgun. So I learned about "lead" on a moving target.

I also learned about ricochet, the bouncing of a projectile off an object, causing the projectile to fly where it shouldn't. This was a very common hazard with the slingshot, as with the rifle, and sometimes led to unfortunate consequences.

I once stalked an English sparrow perched in a willow tree not far from a window of the United Church. When I released the rock it missed the sparrow, bounced off the trunk of the willow, and drove cleanly through the glass up near the apex of the Gothic arch. The glass didn't shatter, but a neat hole just the size of the rock appeared, with cracks radiating out from it.

See what I mean?

Every time I attended Sunday School thereafter, my eyes were drawn irresistibly to that hole in the window. I lived in mortal fear that my sin would be found out, and indeed, God must have known about it, but He never informed the minister.

A Rod and a River

❖   ❖   ❖

I STILL REMEMBER THE FIRST cutthroat trout I caught. I was probably seven years old, and had come by a cast-off tubular steel rod complete with a rusty level-wind reel, a length of braided linen Cuttyhunk line, and three feet or so of heavy catgut leader.

The high water in the Kootenay that spring had carried out a section of Sjoholm's hay meadow just above the highway bridge. One of my brothers suggested I might catch a fish in the resultant back-eddy.

One afternoon when school was out, I made my way across the bridge to the eddy, catching a fine big grasshopper on my way. I threaded him on my hook, whereupon he spread his black-and-yellow wings wide, and I flung him into the eddy.

The Cuttyhunk line always floated until it soaked up water. The 'hopper floated too, so it was like fishing with a dry fly.

There was a silvery glimmer deep in the water below the 'hopper, and a beautiful trout rose and engulfed the bait, right on the surface. I felt the tug and wriggle of that beautiful fish, gave a tremendous yank, and immediately he was struggling and writhing on the grass behind me.

Wow! He was still wiggling when I was halfway home. He was probably ten or twelve inches long, but the thrill he gave me couldn't be duplicated today by anything less than a thirty-pound Kamloops.

This was the first of many chunky cutthroats I took. Of course there were many other species in the river. There were huge Dolly Varden, which we called char, and equally huge ling (burbot). At certain times of year, the Rocky Mountain whitefish (we called them grayling) schooled in unbelievable numbers in the shallow water directly below the highway bridge. We used to fish for them off the bridge, letting long lines down to the water, our small hooks baited with gobs of dough made from flour and water. These fish were not considered good eating, being very bony, but it was a fine pastime for kids.

One day a group of us lined up on the bridge, fishing in this fashion, when suddenly the grayling all disappeared as if by magic. This meant that a big char was about to appear, cruising along in hopes of catching a straggling grayling. Sure enough, a long, dark shape came slowly up from the depths of the main river. Soon we could see his white-edged fins, his white-lined mouth gaping as he sucked in the oxygen-laden water. We were looking down into five or six feet of clear water, so he showed up against the stony bottom with startling clarity.

We had never known one of these big fish to take a dough bait, but this one may have been really hungry. He swam leisurely up to the bait on the end of Einar Johnson's line and took it in. He was much too huge to yard up to the bridge, as we had been doing with the grayling, and we expected him to break off promptly.

For some reason the fish didn't run and Einar didn't

panic. He simply held the line tight while we watched the big char turning and writhing below us. After a long time the fish was exhausted to the point where Einar could draw him to the water's edge below the end of the bridge. One of the other boys clambered down the rocks and lifted the prize out onto the bank. He weighed seven pounds on Baldy Martinos's grocery scales. Truly a great feat for an eleven-year-old, especially with half a dozen admiring spectators.

An afternoon's fishing in some of the many eddies and backwaters would usually yield three or four cutthroats or small char for each of us. We used minnows or tough chunks of beef for bait on fairly large japanned hooks.

We were fishing late one warm summer's evening. I had moved considerably ahead of the rest. Dusk was settling in rapidly, the dark spruces and thick willow growth rendering the setting a bit spooky to a young boy.

There was a big deep hole in front of me, with a good-sized driftwood log against the shore. As I studied the water, a big char swam slowly past. I was sure he saw me with his staring baleful eyes, and a chill ran up my back. Here was a predator on the prowl, and I had the feeling that he was going to come slithering over the log and grab me by the leg. I backed up the bank right smartly.

In a few seconds I regained my courage, and dropped my bait over the log. This time I didn't see the fish. He just seized my hook and took off for the other side of the river. The power of that fish was unbelievable. He simply yanked my rod into the water, ran my line out to the end, popped it without hesitating, and continued on his way. He may as well have been a submarine for all the effect my tackle had.

Another time I was with John Scanland and his father up near the mouth of Bull River. All three of us were standing looking at a big hole we were going to fish, when a great grey shape came up the river. Again we saw the telltale white-edged fins of a monster char. He looked as long as my leg.

Mr. Scanland dropped a minnow-baited hook in front of him. Without pausing the fish took the minnow and continued up the river.

Unfortunately Mr. Scanland's tackle had a fixed line, so he was unable to play the fish in the usual manner. When the char came up against solid resistance he barely rocked. The rod tip came down into the water, the line twanged, and he was gone without even changing his speed. Twenty pounds? Thirty pounds? I don't know, and after all these years I won't even hazard a guess.

We used to set night-lines, too, and the victims of this technique were usually ling. Twenty feet or so of heavy line, a big hook baited with minnow or beef, were all the equipment needed. Tie the end of the line to a stout limb or a big rock, throw the bait and sinker out into an eddy, come back next morning, and chances were good that we would pull out a ling, sometimes four or five pounds in weight. We didn't eat these delicious creatures. The Chinese in town paid up to twenty-five cents for a good ling, and twenty-five cents bought a lot of goodies at Martinos's store.

One lad of twelve caught a huge ling in the big eddy below the railway bridge. With his hand in the gills over his shoulder, the tail of the fish dragged on the ground behind him as he walked home.

Fishing was at its best in May, between breakup and high water. During high water it was a waste of time. But as the water level dropped in early August, fishing picked up again, getting progressively better as the water lowered until freeze-up in the fall.

Sometimes we would get clear ice on the river before

the snow came. Armed with a sledge hammer, a single-bit ax, or simply a boulder, we would walk the clear ice until we found a fish below us. Three or four of us would herd him into shallow water and bring our weapons down hard on the ice, whereupon our victim would turn belly-up, stunned by the concussion. We had to move quickly to chop or otherwise break a hole in the ice, to get the fish before he recovered and swam away.

There was a lake a few hours' hike from Wardner called Number Two Lake. Our schoolteacher and scout master, Bayard Iverson, used to take some of us on weekend trips to that lake to fish for cutthroat trout. It was there that Iverson introduced us to the pleasures of fly-fishing.

The lake was manmade, a dammed-up swampy area on Little Sand Creek. The dam had a chute constructed in such a way that, by removing a few boards, the flow of the creek and consequently the level of the water in the lake could be easily controlled. The swamp had originally been a peat bog. With the rising water, much of the peat around the edges floated free of the bottom, with probably a four-foot depth of water underneath. We could walk out on this surface, feeling the peat undulating as we walked.

Sneaking very cautiously to the edge, we would drop a Royal Coachman with a single salmon egg impaled on it over the edge. The trout liked to lie just under the edge, and as often as not we were rewarded by an immediate strike. Occasionally we hooked trout of up to three pounds in this fashion, and the battles we had with these comparative monsters were thrilling in the extreme. Most of the big ones managed to tangle our lines in roots and break off.

There were a few beavers living in the lake. We found that if we broke their dam at the outlet about noon, the trout in the lake were driven into a feeding frenzy as the water level fell. That night the beavers would repair the dam, and the lake would fill again, lowering the volume in the creek below. This in turn drove the fish in the creek into a frenzy. We would fish the creek in the morning, tear out the dam about noon, and fish the lake in the afternoon. Usually each of us would stagger home on Sunday afternoon with heavy creels. I don't remember what the daily catch limit was then, but whatever it was, we had it.

Pat and Mike

❖   ❖   ❖

"SONNY" JOHNSTON AND I were barely out of the wet-nose stage. His foster father, George Huddleston, had helped us backpack away up the Skookumchuck River. At least it seemed a long way to us. It was our first camping trip on our own. On our way in we saw a big bear working on a rock slide, the first grizzly I ever saw.

Mr. Huddleston left us there with some fishing gear, grub and blankets. We would stay up there for three days, then find our way out as best we could.

The first day we had a ball. Beautiful green pools were loaded with hungry cutthroat trout and char. As fast as we could fling in a grasshopper-loaded hook we pulled out a trout anywhere from a foot to eighteen inches long.

We went to bed that night almost in a state of shock: weary, dirty, and yes, hungry. We didn't know how to cook! We had no tent, of course, since we couldn't have packed one. It was a long time before we fell asleep. Each little rustle in the brush reminded us of the grizzly we had seen.

In the morning Sonny went down to the river for water while I built a fire. It was chilly in the shade of the

great mountain to the east, but it was going to be another
hot August day.

Sonny came running back up to camp with the water
pail empty and in a great state of excitement.

"The river's gone dry!"

"Aw, quit kidding and get some water up here!"

"No, I mean it. The river's nearly dry, and all full
of mud!"

I listened and couldn't hear rushing waters.
Together we hurried down through the fringe of willows
screening the river from our camp. Sonny was right. The
riverbed *was* nearly dry. What little water still coursed
through the boulders was yellow with mud. There were still
some pools and they, too, were thick with silt.

"What do you suppose happened?" Sonny asked.

"Beats me," I answered. "Must be a big landslide
up above that blocked the river right off!"

"Let's go up and have a look!"

We grabbed some bread, smeared it with jam, and
with bread in one hand, fishing rods in the other, started off
upriver. We slipped and slithered over the wet, muddy
boulders in the river channel, hurrying as best we could.
There was so little water in the channel that we could cross
from side to side almost without wetting our feet. The deeper
pools where we had fished the day before still held considerable water. We thought they should be full of stranded
fish, and no doubt they were, but the mud was so thick we
couldn't see beneath the surface.

About a mile above our camp we found the slide. It
couldn't be called a mud slide, because the material was dry,
a mixture of gravel and, mostly, sand. It seemed the whole
side of the mountain had broken off and slid down, completely blocking the river. The face of the slide towered

perhaps a hundred feet above our heads and we had to crane our necks to see the top.

We stood on the opposite side of the channel on a logjam, away from the sheer immensity of it. It seemed apparent that the spring flood had deposited the logjam on the inside of the bend and forced the water to gnaw away at the foot of the mountain, undermining it until it gave way. Even as we watched, lesser slides broke off and came tumbling down, each one stirring up a cloud of dust. But they were insignificant in comparison to what had happened during the night.

"Wish we could see a big chunk come down," I said.

"Yeah, boy, wouldn't that be something!" Sonny answered.

We studied the slide for a while. Thousands of tons of the sandy gravel had come down. A huge pool was forming above the dam, and the muddy water was eddying slowly, with much debris floating on the top. The dam itself was laced with a tangle of trees and brush that had been the cover-growth on the mountainside.

"Hey," Sonny suggested finally, "we might as well go on up the river and do some fishing."

The water had risen so much that we had to work our way through the thick willows well above the level of the regular channel. Above the next bend we found the river to be its usual clear, cool self again. We fished a couple of pools, but we had forgotten our grasshoppers and the trout were not interested in anything we had to offer.

We moved on to a narrow, rocky canyon with some tremendous, deep pools. There should have been some large char lurking in them, and we wished we could catch a mouse or a chipmunk for bait. And then I had a sudden thought.

"Say, you know something? When that dam busts

loose the water is going to tear down the river and wash our camp out. Another thing, we're on the wrong side of the river, and we won't be able to cross back!"

"Holy mackerel, that's right. We better get right back and move our stuff higher up the bank!"

We hurried back down to the head of the pool. The water level had risen considerably. It must be nearly ready to burst over the crest of the dam, and we had a long way to go back to camp.

A dry, limby jack pine of good size was just awash at the water's edge. Sonny waded out and sat on it. It was big enough to float him, but not both of us. With the limbs acting as outriggers it was quite stable, and Sonny shoved off hollering, "See you down at the dam!"

The water was eddying slowly clockwise, and Sonny and his "raft" moved down toward the dam quite close to shore. In the meantime I had to struggle through the willow thicket on the opposite side, wishing I'd had Sonny's forethought.

When I came to the jam below the slide, Sonny was standing on the opposite shore directly below the sheer face where his raft had grounded. Without a pole to manipulate it, he had been forced to abandon ship. The water was all but running over the top of the dam, and Sonny was going to have to move quickly to get over to my side before it let go. Also he was in an extremely hazardous position with thousands of tons of unstable material hanging over him. He started over the dam.

He was about halfway over. I had my neck craned, watching the top of the slide. A big dead tamarack spike stood tight on the brink. Even as I watched, it toppled in slow motion. The bank below it gave way. Suddenly the whole mountainside seemed to be moving.

Sonny started to run while I watched in horror. Dust boiled up, obscuring the scene. A terrible rumble filled the air. Then a wall of gravel about forty feet high came rolling out of the dust. With some vague notion that the brush would hold the slide back, I turned and plunged into the willows.

Sonny had turned down the side of the dam to the muddy channel below. I turned my head for a quick look just as I hit the brush. He was down on hands and knees, scrabbling along apparently in pain. The big tamarack was rolling along right at his heels. Tons of sand and gravel were thundering along, pushing the tamarack before it.

Then I was in the willows, running, heedless of the stinging slaps from the branches on my face, jumping windfalls like a frightened deer. After about fifty yards of this I realized that the roar of the slide had subsided. But what of Sonny?

"Sonny!" I called. . . . No answer.

Again, "SONNY! . . ."

A hellish predicament! Sonny somewhere under a million tons of sand and gravel, probably ground into hamburger by the big tamarack. Me alone, not knowing for sure the way back home. Not only that, but when I was alone I was scared of the dark. And a big grizzly loose somewhere nearby! It was going to be a long, lonesome night.

" . . . SONNEEE! ! . . ."

More frightened than I had ever believed possible, I made my way back to the channel's edge. Out in the mud, sitting on the big tamarack rubbing his leg, was Sonny! With a mixture of relief and anger, I rushed over to him.

"Why in hell didn't you answer when I called? I thought for sure you were dead! Are you all right?"

"Bad cramp in my leg," he answered with a grimace. "I guess my legs froze up, hanging in the water when I was riding the windfall."

I could see the slither marks in the mud where he had crawled ahead of the tamarack. The trees stopped less than twenty feet from where he had been when the action subsided.

I was getting madder by the second. "At least you could have answered me!"

"I was just sitting here thinking," he said.

"Thinking? About what?"

"About you running for the brush when I stayed in the open."

Sonny was a great one for telling jokes. "Did I ever tell you the one about Pat and Mike walking along the railroad track when a train came along?"

"Yeah, I know. Pat said, 'If it caught me in the open what would it have done to me in the brush?' " I had an awful urge to commit murder right then. Just in time I remembered I was afraid of the dark.

With the fresh material on the dam we had plenty of time to get back to camp and move to higher ground. It was nearly four hours later that the dam finally gave way, but it must have gone gradually. Instead of the great rush of water we had expected, the water came up only a couple of feet above its previous level, and by the following morning it was once again clear and green.

We made our way back to Skookumchuck that day, getting lost only once, in a swamp, when we attempted a shortcut over a big ridge. The people who lived along the river had been puzzled as to why the river had gone dry. We were able to boast that we had been eyewitnesses to the cause.

The Beckoning Hills

❖ ❖ ❖

IT WAS MARCH, 1930. The little town of Wardner was in the doldrums. The young men of the town had been laid off work and had amused themselves throughout the winter with reading, playing rummy, whist, crib, and a new card game called bridge. They had spent many hours flooding, scraping, and shoveling snow off the outdoor skating rink. But now they were sick of the sight of books and playing cards. The rink was finished for the year, and it was too early for tennis, baseball, and football. What to do?

The snow was receding from the foothills between Wardner and the Rockies, and the hills beckoned. "Come up and visit us," they seemed to call. "We'll show you a time you won't soon forget. . . ."

My older brothers, Oscar and Ole, and their friend, Jack Moore, decided the call couldn't be ignored. They loaded an old Model T Ford with grub, some other basic camping gear, and sleeping bags they had made for themselves of wool batts covered with blue denim.

Each took a rifle, too, although they couldn't have given a rational reason. The bears were not yet out of hibernation, and the only other game in season was coyotes, for which they had no earthly use.

They took an old bush road that had once serviced some of the logging camps in the hills to the east. Deer were plentiful. They saw dozens of them on the slopes above the road, where they awaited the greening grass.

The Model T rattled past the abandoned site of Camp Seven, but soon the young men began encountering occasional snowdrifts. By the time they reached Camp Seventeen they were constantly in snow. The old Ford had just about had it. No matter. They abandoned the car, loaded their belongings on packboards, and struck off eastward on foot. They had no idea where they were going, but it was enough just to be going.

As they climbed higher into the hills they encountered more snow. It was crusted, as spring snow usually is, and they found the going hard. The crust would bear their weight for two or three steps then suddenly give way, dropping them through to their hips with a jolt. By evening they had made their way down into the great draw at Long Lake, past which the Galloway logging road now runs.

In the meadow at the north end of the lake they found a big stack of slough hay. Some farmer had cut and piled it the summer before, but had never hauled it away. It was an ideal spot for an overnight camp. They built a fire, and while one of them started supper, the other two burrowed into the stack and laid out the sleeping bags.

The night was cold. A brilliant moon and millions of stars floated slowly overhead. Coyotes yammered from the hills as they chased deer through the crusty snow. Occasionally the breeze drifted the smell of their fire into their snug abode. They were tired but content. They slept heavily.

They were up early the next morning and had a fine breakfast of bacon, eggs, and hotcakes, chased down with

coffee brewed from melted snow. They sat around the fire
for a bit, trying to decide what to do with the day. They had
come as far as they could eastward, unless they climbed the
mountain just above their camp.

Climb a mountain? Of course. Jutting out from the
main bulk of the mountain was a huge promontory called
Buffalo Head. From the base to the top would be a climb of
about a thousand feet. The slope was very steep, about the
same as an ordinary house roof. There were no cliffs on the
face. There would be four to five feet of snow at the summit,
covering all the rocks and windfalls. The face had been
burned off in a fierce forest fire the year before, leaving only
a few scattered snags standing. Aside from the snags the
face was completely barren, like a modern ski slope.

They left their camping gear at the haystack, taking
only their rifles. The climb was stiff from the camp to a
bench at the toe of the promontory, and served to warm
them up for the main assault. The crusty snow had hardened
during the night, and they were able to walk right on top.
When they started up the main slope they found it was
necessary to beat out footholds with their rifle butts to keep
from slipping back on their slick-soled rubbers.

Soon they had gained enough altitude to look down
on the surrounding hills, whence they had come. They were
aware that if they were to slip on the heavy crust, they would
slide at terrific speed back to the bottom. To crash into one
of the standing snags would be certain death.

As they climbed, they took turns in the lead, breaking footholds through the crust. When they paused for rest,
each one broke out a space for himself where he could sit.
They were being very, very careful.

Oscar was in the lead when they finally reached the
top. There was just a slight slope where Oscar stepped

forth on the crust, believing it to be safe. He was wrong. In a second he was flat on his back, sliding back over the face.

His first thought was to straddle his rifle and use it to break through the crust. The crust was hard as flint, and the rifle butt made no impression. In a heartbeat he was flying down the terrifying slope, completely out of control. It was all he could do to keep his feet pointed downhill, to keep from revolving as he slid. Below, the menacing black snags waited for him.

It's not possible to estimate the speed he must have reached. On such a steep slope, on what amounted to glare ice, it was almost a free-fall. And a thousand feet to the bottom, studded with the burned snags!

The mountainside was a bit concave, a very wide, shallow swale. Oscar didn't slide in a straight line. Rather, he crossed back and forth in a series of great swoops. The snags flashed by one by one, blurred with the speed.

To Ole and Jack, watching in horror from above, it seemed inevitable that Oscar would hit one of the snags and be torn limb from limb. From their vantage point the scene was foreshortened. The snags seemed to be thickly grouped. In reality they were pretty well separated, but even so, there was little likelihood that Oscar would escape them all.

Oscar had a sensation of flying. Several times he saw that he was heading directly toward a snag, but some little irregularity in the ground would send him swooping to one side or the other.

With the quick loss in elevation the crust weakened near the bottom, and finally his rifle butt broke through. He braked to a stop.

Terribly shaken, he looked back up to the two tiny figures at the top and waved his arms to signify that he was all right. They waved back.

He gathered wood and built a big fire. Only when it was going well did the reaction set in. He had had a terrifying experience and trembled for a long while. He was to find, too, that a long time would pass before he could stand on a high point, even on bare ground, without vertigo.

It took Ole and Jack two hours to climb down on foot; Oscar had come down in less than a minute on the seat of his pants. Enough was enough. They made their way back to the haystack camp, spent the night there, and next day resurrected the Ford for the ride back to Wardner.

The hills had promised a time they wouldn't soon forget, and they never did.

Living Off the Land

❖ ❖ ❖

WE LIVED THROUGH THE last half of the Great Depression on a farm near Ta-Ta Creek, some forty miles north of Wardner. To a great many people these years were very hard and best forgotten, but to me they were the best years of my life.

I was sixteen when we moved to Ta-Ta Creek. I had finished my formal education by scraping through grade eight, and I was young enough that I didn't have any responsibilities, so I was carefree.

There were several of us living on the farm. My sister, Teresia, with two young children to care for, was in charge of the kitchen. As the youngest of our little commune, I was delegated to help her with the endless drudgery she faced. But there was not all that much I could do to help her, and I found myself with a lot of leisure time. What better way to spend it than to roam the hills with gun in hand, reliving in imagination the lives of the great woodsmen of the early days?

As far as food went we lived very well, with any amount of milk, butter, eggs, cream, and the vegetables we grew by the ton but couldn't sell. We had a few cows that we hoped to build into a beef herd one day. We hesitated to kill any of our few breeding animals, and the odd steer we butchered went to eke out our scanty cash reserves.

Meat, then, was our greatest concern. Of course we had chickens, but believe me, an unremitting diet of chicken soon palls. The same goes for eggs.

A few years before, great forest fires had swept through the hills from Cherry Creek on the south to Canal Flats on the north, and transformed the forest to grassland. Deer had multiplied at an astonishing rate with the fresh browse that sprang up in the wake of the fires. Meat? The hills were full of it for the taking. On many an evening there would be up to a dozen deer feeding in our alfalfa field. The temptation was not to be denied, nor was our need.

Because of my leisure time I became the hunter. It's most commonly called poaching. A kinder term would be "living off the land." Call it what you will, nearly every farmer we knew in those days did it. Many of the staunch conservationists I know today were inveterate poachers then.

The population in the East Kootenays was not nearly what it is today, so there was not much hunting pressure on the game. There were no elk around Ta-Ta Creek then, and without competition for range the deer flourished. I seldom encountered another hunter in the woods. In fact, I hunted for at least two seasons without meeting another hunter. Thus the deer we killed in our region were relatively few.

The game wardens knew very well what was going on, but they turned a blind eye unless someone was killing wantonly, or for sale. I recall one year when three of us, all young men, spent the winter in a decrepit old cabin in the hills west of Ta-Ta Creek. One day in January I killed two deer just up the draw from the cabin, dragged them down, and hung them at the side of the shack. One was for our use, the other destined for the table at the farm.

The following afternoon the game warden from Cranbrook snowshoed up to our door. We had a fine big kettle of stew bubbling on the stove, and as hospitality dictated we asked him to share a meal with us. Even though his nostrils quivered a bit at the rich scent of the stew, he declined, saying he had just finished his lunch.

He inquired whether there were many coyotes around, took my rifle down from its peg on the wall and inspected it, drank a cup of coffee, and departed without mentioning the freshly killed deer or the bloody drag-marks in the snow.

We knew of one family who found the times particularly hard. They did their poaching in a rather unusual manner. They had no firearms, so they had to improvise.

On a neighboring farm there was a haystack in an isolated meadow. The stack was surrounded by a high wire fence to protect it from hungry deer during the winter months when feed was scarce. Two of the family's teenage boys cut a hole in the fence, and at night would set a snare of telephone wire in the opening. They would retire to a quiet spot up the side-hill until they heard a deer struggling in the snare, then would rush down to the deer, drag it into the bush along a little creek nearby, and kill it there. They would then repair the hole in the fence and repeat the performance when they were again in need of meat.

Although I was out rambling in the hills nearly every day, I wasn't always hunting. I suppose you could say I was communing with nature. Almost every time I went out, there was much of interest to see, and the more I saw, the more observant I became. I often saw the never-ending drama of life and death.

I sometimes watched expert stalkers at work, such as a weasel pursuing and capturing a gopher, or a falcon swooping down on a sharp-tailed grouse several times his size. One day I came upon a battleground where two black bears had fought to the death, the larger one killing the smaller and then feeding on the body. The big one was an old enemy of ours, and I in turn killed him when he returned for another meal. Such are the laws of nature, the dominant species preying on the weaker.

On the other hand, I once watched a big whitetail buck breed a doe, and here I saw the replenishing of a species.

When reading accounts of the great trackers of the past, I concentrated on learning all I could of that skill. And I did become fairly proficient. One of the outfitters I worked for in later years once told the hunter I was to guide that "Fee can track a chipmunk across a rock slide." I think he was exaggerating a little.

One spring day I picked up the tracks of a small bear up on the north slope of Lost Dog Mountain. I had no wish to kill him, but here was a fine opportunity to test my skill. The ground was hard for the most part, and covered with duff and small brush. But the gullies were still damp with the spring runoff, and by circling and searching these damp places I was able to follow him for a couple of miles.

I was surprised when I finally caught up with him. I had thought of him as a black bear, but he turned out to be brown. This showed me that I was not paying attention to small details. Somewhere along the back-trail I should have noticed a few brown hairs. I had been studying the obvious and ignoring the rest. A good lesson.

Another time I wounded a whitetail buck in the snow. Tracking him by the blood trail was easy, of course, but darkness came on before I caught up with him, and I was forced to abandon the hunt for the day.

Early next morning I was back on the track. I found where the buck had bedded down for a long time, and when he moved on he had stopped bleeding. There was one oddity about his tracks, however. His right hind foot turned out just a bit, and by this clue I pursued him across dozens of other tracks. Late in the afternoon I killed him in a dense tangle of windfalls. The original wound had been slight, the bullet just barely breaking the skin on the bottom of his brisket. I doubt that it had even been painful, and certainly he would have recovered with no ill effects. But it was always our rule never to leave wounded game to suffer, and I had pursued him into the second day to live up to that rule.

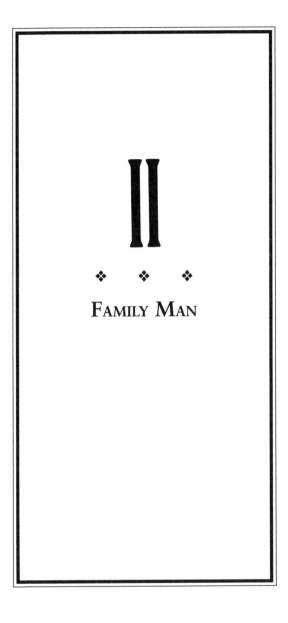

II

FAMILY MAN

Love Story

❖　❖　❖

I WAS TWELVE YEARS OLD when I fell in love.

She was an extremely pretty little ten-year-old, with long black hair, shining dark eyes, and a cute little scar on her chin that I learned was caused by her running into a barbed wire fence in the dark. She even had a pretty name — Alta.

Times were hard then, it being the beginning of the Great Depression. Since she had five brothers and two sisters, her family was finding things even more difficult than most. Her father ran the road grader for the Department of Highways, but the pay was poor and work was not steady. Her mother was a frail, thin woman, already showing the effects of child-bearing and the drudgery of caring for a large family.

Years later Alta told me a story that reflects the desperation of the times and their situation. They had a big, black, good-for-nothing dog. Good for nothing, that is, except that he dispensed a lot of love. The children, of course, loved him in return.

The government at the time paid a four-dollar bounty on coyotes. There were a lot of them in the hills but they were very hard to hunt. It was necessary to put out bait to fetch them within gunshot range. Alta's father in desperation decided that Curley was the only bait available. He was not only useless, but he ate a lot.

Accordingly, one morning he tied a rope to Curley's neck, took rifle in hand, and strode off across the field with Curley fighting the rope and looking back toward the children, who watched in agony.

They could not bear to hear the sound of the shot that would signal Curley's demise, so they covered their ears for what seemed a long, long time. Finally, believing that it must be over, they uncovered their ears and ran to the door in the forlorn hope that they would see Curley coming back home across the field. They reached the door just in time to hear the flat crack of the rifle echo down from the hills.

A couple of mornings later the father collected a four-dollar coyote from Curley's remains.

This little story, of course, has nothing to do with our romance, except perhaps to help introduce why Alta was so appealing to me. Each morning she walked three miles to school. In the afternoon she walked back. Since she was the oldest child, she had to help her mother with the housework and the endless labor connected to the welfare of the younger children, including washing diapers. She didn't scream and shriek like other girls of her age. She didn't step on our marbles or run off with our baseball. In other words, she was much more quiet and mature than the others.

Besides, she was very, very pretty.

What I felt for that girl is called puppy love. Just about everyone suffers through it but eventually recovers. I never did. I decided, privately of course, that I was going to marry that pretty little girl.

Chips Off the Old Block

❖   ❖   ❖

In 1941 I married the pretty little brunette.

In a few years Alta and I were parents to one daughter and three sons. Lynn was not much interested in the outdoor life, but the boys took to it with gusto. Bryan was our firstborn. From the time he was able to toddle I took him with me, and pointed out the fascinating things in the realm of nature. I followed suit with the other boys in their turns.

I would walk them out into the hills as far as they could manage, doing everything I could to confuse them as to direction, and when we were some way from home I would ask them in which direction they thought home lay. From the first it was nearly impossible to confuse Bryan. He seemed to have a homing instinct like a pigeon.

At eight he shot his first elk — a big, bony cow — with his Red Ryder BB gun. He had walked alone four or five miles through bear-infested wilderness up to the sawmill where I worked, and as we were on our way home in the crew truck that afternoon a big cow stood at the side of the road. She was used to the passing of the truck, and stood about seventy feet away waiting for us to go by. Albert

Carolei was driving the truck, and he stopped beside the cow.

"Shoot her, Bryan," he said, "right behind the shoulder." Of course he knew that the pellet from the BB gun would not hurt her. Bryan poked his gun out the window and pulled the trigger. The old cow hunched her back and ran off into the brush, surprised and indignant.

Bryan was fourteen when he first hunted big game seriously. That first day he killed a fine four-point whitetail buck, and a couple of hours later, a fat mule deer doe. The following year he took his first elk, a spike.

On that day he demonstrated his sense of direction. He had shot the elk late in the afternoon, gutted it, and left it for recovery later. It was dark by the time he rejoined his companions where they waited beside their truck. He had crossed another road some time before killing the elk. Since that road passed much closer to the kill than the one they were on, he suggested they drive around by it to recover the meat. And so they struck off in the darkness through country devoid of landmarks, and from the opposite direction. Bryan walked ahead, while his two companions grumbled that he could never find the elk in the darkness. They were just ready to call to Bryan that they should give up, when they caught up to him sitting on the elk.

Gary, our second son, killed a goat one fine fall day when he was thirteen. He had accompanied me into some high country on the Wild Horse River, where we isolated a lone goat on the face of a cliff. I offered him my .270 Husqvarna, knowing I could get the goat should he miss or wound him. Gary didn't miss.

He set bowling pins in the old Venezia Hotel bowling alley until he earned forty dollars, enough money to buy himself a .30-.06 Enfield military rifle, which he affectionately named Ol' George. Now, some twenty-five years later, he still packs this unwieldy old club in preference to any modern scope-sighted rifle. Nearly all the game he has killed with it has been shot through either the neck or the head. He is the most successful hunter of us all.

When Gary was fifteen and sixteen he spent part of each summer vacation camped by himself at Many Waters Campground on the Wild Horse in one of my tepees. We would help him set up camp with a supply of grub, a sleeping bag, and other necessary paraphernalia, and there he would spend a week or more, climbing into the high basins each morning, exploring the surrounding wild country as far as he could go in a day's travel. We never worried. The only stipulation we made was that each morning when he left camp he must enter in a log where he intended to travel that day. In the unlikely event of catastrophe we would know where to look for him.

Every two or three evenings we would drive up with fresh grub and clean clothes. One night when we were late in getting to his camp, we chased a porcupine out of the tepee before he woke up.

He climbed and crawled all over the peaks and canyons in the area until he had a thorough knowledge of every one. Of course he was not hunting with intent to kill on these summer jaunts; there was so much wildlife to see, so much beautiful alpine country to explore, that these glories were more than enough in themselves.

Perhaps I should remark here that our hunting requirements had changed from the days of the Depression. No longer were we so dependent on wild meat. Still, the meat we garnered in the fall hunting season was an important part of our economy. Now, with our boys contributing, and with the advent of the refrigerator and freezer, we had plenty of legally killed game to supply our needs. And our hunts were not always successful. Naturally, the successful hunts are the ones we tell about, but there were many, many days when we returned home weary and empty-handed to a supper of "track soup."

Ray, our fourth child in succession (that's rapid succession — he was just five years younger than Bryan), collected two mule deer bucks on his first day of hunting with a rifle. He was with Bryan on that day, up in Two-Buck Basin at the head of the Wild Horse. While Bryan sat scanning the basin through his binoculars, Ray whispered, "I hear something coming." And a moment later, "There's a buck!"

Without lowering his binoculars Bryan whispered back, "Shoot him!"

...Pow! "Got him!" Ray said. Then, "There's another one!"

"Shoot him too," Bryan responded, "but in the head."

...Pow! "Got him, too!" Ray said with satisfaction.

At two o'clock that afternoon they were back in camp, Bryan with one whole deer on his packboard, Ray with the hindquarters of the second. After coffee, they climbed back up into that huge basin for the front quarters they had left behind.

I had long prided myself on my ability to pack heavy loads for long distances over rugged terrain. All three of the boys took to backpacking with the same pride. One fall morning we were camped at the Big Slide Campground on the Wild Horse. Bryan elected to hunt the range to the east, while Gary, Ray, and Ray's good friend, Brian Piwick, climbed the range to the west. Since I was sure some of the boys would be successful, I lolled around camp with Alta.

Dale Piwick was with us, too, and he hunted up along the creek bottom.

Bryan crossed the height of land some two thousand feet above our camp, over into the Bull River watershed. Down at timberline on that side he killed a two-point mule deer. He gutted it, put the whole carcass on his packboard, and packed it back over the summit and down to the horse trail on Anderson Creek on the Wild Horse side. He had a terrific headache, so he left the deer there on the trail, intending to come back for it the next day, and returned to camp about one o'clock in the afternoon.

Gary, Ray, and Brian Piwick, meanwhile, had climbed up past timberline on the west side of the valley. Here Gary began to feel ill, so he returned to camp. Ray and Brian Piwick opted to keep going to the higher country, thinking that they might get a bighorn ram. They were only fourteen years old, and shouldn't have been hunting without an adult companion.

They stopped for lunch on a huge promontory high above the valley floor. Below them was a typical alpine basin with the usual small stream coursing through it. Above them was a long shale slope crisscrossed with numerous game trails. They thought a band of sheep might come along one of these trails or appear in the basin below.

All at once they heard a piercing whistle from the spruce timber far below them. It came from away down the mountain, close by the logging road. Neither had heard such a sound before, but they knew it must be the bugle of a bull elk.

Ray was carrying my elk bugle in his pocket. Pulling it out, he gave an approximation of the sound. The bull squealed back a time or two, then seemed to lose interest. It was cold in the wind on their promontory, so they decided to drop down into the basin to finish their lunch.

Down there they were much more comfortable, in the sun and out of the wind. Ray tooted away on the bugle a time or two, and the elk answered again. He sounded much closer. Then he broke off again, and the boys thought he had again lost interest. The next thing they knew, he bugled a great blast from the fringe of timber close by. Ray was carrying a .303 British Lee Enfield rifle with a brass butt plate, and he bashed the butt in the rocks. Immediately the bull set up such a clamor in the brush that it frightened the boys. There was a huge boulder lying beside the little stream, and the boys sought cover behind it.

Ray gave one more call on the whistle, and the elk came roaring out into the clearing, screaming and thrashing his antlers. Every hair on his body stood on end; his eyes bulged and rolled in his head, showing the whites. The two boys were all but panic-stricken. They both fired and the elk collapsed on the spot. Later examination showed that one bullet had struck the bull through the heart; the other had broken his neck.

Neither boy had gutted anything larger than a fish, although they had seen it done. Here they were confronted by this huge animal that it took the two of them to roll over. They took turns cutting delicately at the carcass, careful not to cut a gut. It took them two hours to finish the chore. Following the procedure they had heard about many times, they rolled the carcass up on a couple of poles to drain and cool, covering it loosely with green boughs to discourage birds. Then they trotted back down the mountain to camp, carrying the huge liver and looking for help to pack the meat out.

We were lucky that we had a lot of manpower on that trip. Bryan had already put in a strenuous morning climbing the eastern peaks and packing his buck down to the pack trail on Anderson Creek. Luckily he had brought his packboard back to camp with him. Dale Piwick had returned from his hunt up the creek. Gary was too ill to make the climb, and in any case we were short one pack-board, so the other five of us struck back up the mountain to the elk. It took us two hours of hard climbing to get there, and Ray and Brian were repeatedly chaffed for calling the elk from the vicinity of the road up to timberline.

The animal was huge, the biggest-bodied elk I have ever seen, although his antlers were nothing to brag about. We cut the meat into chunks we felt we could handle, and late in the afternoon began the savage trek back down the mountain through brush and windfalls. By the time we reached the bottom I had mixed feelings. Up until that time I had been the leader, the one who carried the biggest pack, climbed the mountains fastest, led the way in all our adven-tures. But by the time we reached camp, I knew my boys now surpassed me. I staggered the last half mile on rubbery legs, completely exhausted. Later, back home, we weighed Bryan's pack. It weighed one-hundred-and-ten pounds! And remember, that day he had already packed a whole deer over the divide to the east!

During the twenty years since Bryan was born, we had lived first at Ta-Ta Creek, then Marysville, Edgewater, Wilmer, Ta-Ta Creek again, Invermere, Ta-Ta Creek for the third time, then Fort Steele, Waldo, and finally Cranbrook.

All are in the East Kootenay District, second only to Africa in numbers and diversity of big game. And from any of our numerous homes it was just a short walk in to good hunting country. Most of the time we were something less than well off, but in retrospect we wouldn't have had it otherwise.

Our boys had been reared to appreciate this great country from an outdoorsman's point of view, and I felt I had taught them well. And so, on the Day of the Elk, while I felt bad about relinquishing my place as the leader in everything pertaining to the hunt, I felt a great pride in these young men, flesh of my flesh.

Gary and the Raccoon

❖   ❖   ❖

WE SPENT 1949 THROUGH 1951 with our little family in Letcher's logging camp on Gold Creek, twelve miles west of Waldo. We had free housing, such as it was, and there was a school for the children, but the working conditions were the worst I have ever encountered anywhere. It was a terribly hard life for Alta, too. But for our four children, the boys especially, it was plain heaven.

Gold Creek meandered right through the middle of the camp, loaded with hungry trout available to the kids any time they felt like wetting a line. Virgin timber stretched for miles, and the hills were full of wild animals. There was unlimited opportunity for adventure, and the three boys took advantage of these opportunities with gusto.

There was another member of our family, named Bingo. He was a large mongrel with some black-and-tan characteristics, and he was as addicted to adventure as the boys. But Bingo was a little different. He had a lot of common sense, which the boys seemed to lack. Even so, things sometimes went wrong, especially when Bingo was with Gary, who was seven at the time. Gary was a dreamer, blessed (or cursed) with a great deal of imagination. There were times when he suffered for his actions, and as a result he didn't always divulge certain information. Bingo took everything philosophically, probably because he seldom got hammered for any misdeeds performed.

One hot summer afternoon the two of them set out in search of excitement, Gary astride the old three-speed bike that had no brakes and was stuck permanently in high gear. Bingo trotted happily at his side, tongue hanging out below a big grin.

They barely avoided being caught in a serious misdemeanor. Gary had commandeered his older brother's slingshot, and he and Bingo made the two-mile run down to the Chain Lakes. Gary stood at the edge of the water, shooting rocks out into the lake to get the feel of the forbidden weapon. Unfortunately one of the rocks fouled up in the pouch of the slingshot, and when he released it the forward momentum of the rock yanked the crutch out of his hand. It floated about twenty feet offshore, well beyond recovery. Gary stood on the shore in his ragged shorts and worn sneakers, watching the slingshot bob ever farther out with the offshore breeze. So near, and yet so far! Thoughts of the pummeling he would receive at his older brother's hands saddened him considerably.

Bingo sat by his side, ears perked up, not understanding what was wrong but offering in his own dumb way to help. Of course! Bingo loved to retrieve sticks! Gary selected a piece of limb, spat on it, offered it to Bingo to sniff, and flung it out toward the slingshot. Bingo plunged happily into the water, swam out to the stick, and brought it back to Gary. The slingshot floated on. Again Gary threw the stick. Again Bingo retrieved it. Gary tried to tell Bingo that he was supposed to bring in the slingshot, but Bingo didn't comprehend. Time after time he ignored the weapon but brought the stick faithfully back to shore.

Eventually they both grew tired of the stick game. Gary sat morosely on the bank, watching the slingshot float farther and farther away. Finally in exasperation he jumped up and flung a rock at the frustrating item. Bingo leaped into the water, swam out to the splash and, since the rock had sunk, grasped the slingshot in his jaws, brought it in, and deposited it at Gary's feet. Wow! Gary danced a little jig. Bingo had come through again!

On another day when they were a short distance down the logging road toward Waldo a furry grey animal crossed the road ahead of them at great speed, kicking up small clouds of dust at each leap, and climbed up a thickly limbed jack pine. Gary stopped the bike at the foot of the tree. He couldn't think of any animal that resembled this one, except a raccoon. He leaned against the bike and peered up into the tree, but the blazing sun was directly behind the raccoon, rendering it indistinct in the thick limbs.

Bingo was a gentle dog. He wouldn't harm anything unless ordered to do so, but then he was a deadly killer. At first he was indifferent to the raccoon odor, which he must have smelled, but when Gary said, "Sic 'em," he picked up interest and began baying at the foot of the tree.

It came to Gary that he would be a great hero if he could return to camp with a raccoon. This was very appealing, since he rarely rated the hero category. He started climbing the tree, shouting "Sic 'em!" from time to time to keep Bingo on his toes. Bingo waved his tail and shouted back. Up the tree Gary went, the raccoon keeping pace ahead of him until eventually there was no more tree to climb. Then the raccoon jumped.

There was a heap of loosely piled brush near the base of the tree, and the raccoon sought shelter in it. But

Bingo hit the heap with determination and sent the whole thing flying. There were brief sounds of one-sided conflict, and then it was all over.

Success! Gary's heart beat fast with excitement as he scrambled down from the tree and rushed over for his first look at a real raccoon.

Horrors! It was, or had been, Mrs. Letcher's prized tomcat! Gary lived with this guilt on his conscience for thirty years. When he confessed to me just the other day, somehow I couldn't bring myself to give him the thrashing he deserved.

There was a little girl in the camp who seemed to think a lot of Gary. She tormented him unmercifully. One day after school Gary decided he had had enough. He took a handful of stinging nettles and shoved them down the back of her blouse. He didn't come home that afternoon. He struck off up the logging road that came from down near the International Boundary. He had a vague idea that he would be safe once he had crossed the Line.

Fortunately a rancher who lived five miles from the Letchers saw the boy strolling along the road past his hay field. He loaded Gary onto his tractor and gave him a ride back to camp. Of course Gary suffered the usual indignities, but he thought it was well worth it to get a ride on the tractor.

The boys of the newer generation don't seem to have the same flair for adventure that our boys showed. Take Gary's son, Eric, for instance. He showed some signs of talent when, at three, he rode his new tricycle part way down the basement stairs, but lately he has gone in for electronics in a big way.

Too bad.

Bryan's Char

❖   ❖   ❖

BRYAN DROPPED HIS BRASS WOBBLER into the deep water at the head of the pool formed by a beaver dam. We nearly always caught a nice cutthroat trout or two in that hole, and Bryan was anticipating the usual pound to pound-and-a-half trout. What happened gave him the greatest fishing thrill he will likely ever experience. A great Dolly Varden shot out from the tangle of logs at the head of the dam and seized his lure.

Bryan did just what any nine-year-old boy would do under the circumstances. He reared back on the rod, intending to yank the fish out over his head. The big trout was as immovable as the logs. Bryan's line parted with a snap and left him staring at the water in wonder. The sight of that big fish with his fins edged in white, his great mouth slashing at the lure, will remain in Bryan's memory as long as he lives.

Later that same day I enticed the fish to take a small live trout. He took it with Bryan's wobbler still hanging from the corner of his mouth. But he was too much for me, too, with my five-pound test line. He made it into the logs and broke off.

The following week I hung him again, in the same

spot, with the same results. This time he regurgitated a partly digested trout about ten inches long before he broke my line. Some time later we watched him come back and swallow the trout for the second time, and the sight of him cruising around the pool in front of us was grand indeed. I thought he would weigh perhaps ten pounds, and in this small creek with its population of relatively small cutthroats he rated as a monster. To Bryan he must have looked still larger than he did to me.

The following weekend was to be our last attempt at catching him, since we were finally moving from Letchers' camp to Cranbrook.

About noon that day we arrived at the beaver dam, but we were unable to raise the monster from his lair. We thought that, since the water level had dropped considerably, the Big One had probably moved back down the creek to the Kootenay River. We were disappointed, of course. But then I made him out, lying on the bottom in the swift water just above the head of the pool. There must have been a pocket of slack water right on the bottom, and he lay there finning slowly, holding his position, no doubt waiting for some small trout to come down the current.

I tried almost every lure I owned, casting upstream above him and drawing the lure down to him. He ignored every one. In fact, on one cast the lure drifted down and he had to move slightly to one side to let it slip by. Finally I came to my last lure, a creation which had a variety of colored jackets to slip on or off as the situation demanded. I snapped on a fluorescent red jacket and cast it in. This lure ran deep and as I brought it past his snout, it ran right on the bottom, stirring up a faint wake of mud. He opened his mouth and took it in.

We expected him to make the usual rush to the logs,

but to our surprise he simply lay there on the bottom, shaking his head from time to time but apparently in no panic to rid himself of the hooks. Putting all the pressure I dared on my weak line, I could lift him right to the surface, whereupon he would merely tilt his body to catch the power of the water, and plane back down to the bottom.

This was no good. The fish wasn't tiring a bit, and there wasn't much point in standing around on the logjam all afternoon. There was a big treble hook loose in my tackle box, and I instructed Bryan to find a stick to serve as a handle while I stripped out one of my shoelaces.

Bryan lashed the hook to the stick with the lace, and armed with this makeshift gaff, I drew the char to the surface and sank the treble hook into his back just behind his head. The hook simply straightened out. The char, finally shocked out of his lethargy, streaked down the pool. Instead of running into the tangle of logs, however, he passed them and ended up in the lower end of the pool in comparatively shallow water. In doing so, he passed the line under the end of one of the logs.

There was only one way of freeing my line, and I took it. I leaped as far as I could across the deep part of the pool, and landed in water up to my waist. Now I was on the far side of the pool. I reached my rod tip back under the log, and miraculously the line came free.

For the first time our situation looked good. The fish was in about three feet of open water, and I stood in the pool between him and the logs. Now it was just a matter of time. Soon he was floundering weakly on the end of my line. He lay on the surface, gills pumping. The steep, muddy bank was higher than my head here, and I wasn't sure just how we were going to land him. I put one hand under him and gave a heave, trying to fling him to the top where Bryan was dancing with excitement. But he was too heavy. He hit just short of the crest, rolled back into the water, and made one more weak rush.

I told Bryan to find a club and take a position so he could club the fish the next time I flung him up. He found a piece of a big fir limb about the size of a softball bat, and when the fish came up to him he swung with perfect timing right to the head. The fish was ours.

It was only then that I realized I had lost the shoe from which I had taken the lace for the gaff. We had to wait for fifteen minutes for the mud to settle out of the pool so I could recover my shoe.

We estimated his weight at ten pounds. On the bathroom scales at home he went nine and a quarter. Bathroom scales? We settled for an official weight of nine pounds.

On Lassoing Fish

❖   ❖   ❖

ALTA ONCE WON BOTH FIRST and second prizes in a fish derby conducted by the Kimberley Rod and Gun Club. She won both prizes, strangely enough, with one fish. Odd as that may seem, it was nothing to the way she caught the fish.

We're not sure now what year it was, but it must have been somewhere around 1955. My sister, Teresia, her husband, Frank Moore, with their son, Lorne, took us up to Grundy Lake, a few miles east of Wasa, one Sunday in August. It was the first time we had been to the lake. We had no boat, so Alta and I started up the east side of the lake, casting out from the shore with our spinning gear as we went. The Moores did the same on the west side.

A few rainbows were jumping here and there, but there seemed to be nothing big. The lake didn't seem to us likely to hold any big ones, although we had heard the usual rumors of five- and six-pounders having been taken. One fish kept jumping just offshore, time and time again in the same spot. Every few minutes it would come out of the water in a fine leap. It was a nice one, but just out of casting range. Of course we had no way of knowing whether it was the same fish, but we assumed it was.

I'm an impatient fisherman. If a fish doesn't take quickly, I'm inclined to move to another spot. Alta, on the other hand, will spend a lot of time in one place. Perhaps that's why she consistently outfishes me.

She settled down on the edge of the lake in front of this fish, determined to keep after it until it took. Even though she couldn't quite cast to where it was carrying on, she persevered for perhaps ten or fifteen minutes.

I had worked my way some distance along the shore when I heard her shout, and looked over to see her rod bent in a deep arc. Another man was on the other side of her, casting a wobbler as we had been doing, and when he saw that she had a very good fish on, he came up to watch the battle.

Judging by the power the fish displayed, it was not the jumper. It took a long time for Alta to bring it in to where we could get a first glimpse of it. We were disappointed to see that it was not as large as we had thought. Still it was some minutes before Alta subdued it. Apparently it was foul-hooked.

Alta backed up the beach, drawing the fish in, while I stood at the water's edge to assist in landing it. We didn't use a net in those days of plenty, preferring to give the fish that advantage. When I got a good look at Alta's catch I could see that it had a small willow-leaf lure hanging from its mouth. That explained why it kept jumping — in an effort to throw the hook it must have broken off from another angler's line.

When I lifted it in by the willow leaf, we saw that it had been caught in an unbelievable manner. Somehow Alta's lure had passed completely around its body just ahead of the dorsal fin, and the treble hook had caught her line. The fish had been lassoed.

Even though the fish was only a little more than two pounds, Alta entered it in the Ladies Division of the Kimberley Rod and Gun Club competition. And how did she come to win both first and second prizes?

It turned out that this was the only fish entered in that division. Since the club had allotted a certain sum for each of two prizes, they decided to combine the amounts, and they presented her with an expensive Swedish-built spinning reel!

The Fire

❖　　❖　　❖

THIS EVENT HAPPENED BEFORE the days of the women's liberation movement and, although we didn't realize it at the time, was an indication of things to come.

Alta, our son Gary, and I went up to Grundy Lake east of Wasa one Sunday to do a bit of fishing. It was one of our hot summers, with the bush so dry it was crisp as cornflakes. The day in question felt as though the Devil was stoking up for a barbecue.

On our walk from the end of the road to the lake we met three men coming out. We exchanged greetings, and of course inquired about the fishing. They had caught a couple of fish apiece, and one of them showed us a nice two-pounder. Not too bad, considering the heat.

When we arrived at the lake we spotted a column of smoke rising from the far shore. Naturally we hurried around the shoreline to see whether we could contain the fire before it got out of hand. We found a situation that was beyond us but we still had to try.

Many years before, a large tree had fallen across a jumble of the big broken rock typical of that area. Now the tree was nothing but punk, and the punk had fallen down among the boulders. The fire had probably started from a discarded cigarette. It was burning the punk, not blazing but smouldering fiercely and working its way persistently along the line of the tree's fall toward a thicket.

We had no way of moving the big boulders. Thirty feet away was a lake full of water, but there was no way to get the water to the fire.

I had seen two beer bottles on the shore as we came around the lake, no doubt abandoned there by some litter-bug fisherman. Hopeless as it seemed, I ran back to fetch them. We needed to transfer water from the lake to the fire, but it was going to take more water than we could hope to move with two beer bottles. When I returned to the fire, Alta, who is always more resourceful than I, remembered I had a plastic bag in my creel, Kitchen Catcher size. While one of us ran to and fro with a bottle in each hand, another scurried back and forth with the Kitchen Catcher, while the third sat back and caught his or her breath.

Although we held the fire back a little, there was no chance that we could extinguish it. The next step, then, was to get word to the Forestry Department. Alta hiked back to the end of the road, fired up the old Chev, and drove back to the nearest phone at Wasa with the tidings. Gary and I, meanwhile, continued passing water to the fire.

Alta returned and half an hour later three young men arrived with a small portable pump and some hose. We won. One of the Forestry boys very politely took our names and addresses. Leaving them to put the finishing touches to the fire, we headed for home.

It was a good feeling, driving along, a feeling that we had had a successful day even though we hadn't wet a line. We conjectured that there might be an investigation into the cause of the fire, since the Forestry youth had taken our names. There might even be suspicion that we ourselves were to blame.

It was a couple of weeks later that three envelopes arrived in the mail, one to each of us. Gary opened his first. To our surprise there was a time slip and a check made out to Gary, listing him as a "Fire Fighter" at ninety cents per hour for four hours. Mine was the same, but Alta's was in the sum of four dollars at the hourly rate of one dollar, and she was listed as "Foreman." Someone in the Forestry Department had a sense of humor! A secretary, no doubt.

The Prospectors

❖   ❖   ❖

THIS STORY WILL NOT HAVE the impact on my readers that it had on me. To me it was a near thing, although when the rock slide came down I was nearly a mile from it.

There was a time when Bryan and Gary, as well as I, took a keen interest in prospecting for whatever mineral we could find. The fact that we did not find anything of value was beside the point. We spent many interesting days poking around in the rocks, and we did find enough to keep us hopeful. In later years we were to discover a good placer gold prospect, but that is another story.

At the time of this incident, Gary was in the Canadian Air Force stationed in Greenwood, Nova Scotia, so the only time he was actively with us was when he managed to get home on his annual leave. Bryan, too, had many other interests. As a consequence I often found myself climbing around, rock hammer in hand, all alone in the mountains.

Most of our prospecting was done up in the Wild Horse area. The big find on the Wild Horse was the discovery of placer gold in the 1800s. Following the gold rush the hills were literally crawling with prospectors searching for the mother lode, and for silver deposits, of which there was much geological evidence. One eventual result was the discovery of the fabulous Sullivan Mine at the present location of Kimberley. Certainly the entire Wild Horse watershed had been gone over with a fine-tooth comb long before we were even born.

That didn't matter to us. There might be mineral deposits that had been discovered but had little value in that remote time. Once we had reason to believe we had come upon just such a deposit.

Just south of where the East Fork of the Wild Horse branches, we found a talus slope below a huge, beetling crag. It abounded with samples of ore. Tests showed it to be pyrrhotite, a common ore of iron, which sometimes has other valuable ore associated with it. The main ore body at Sudbury, Ontario, for instance, is pyrrhotite with the ore minerals pentlandite (an iron-nickel sulphide) and chalcopyrite embedded in it. The mine at Sudbury is a tremendously important source of nickel.

We staked four claims, naming the group the Gail M in honor of Gary's bride.

One day we picked up a hitchhiker and invited him to come to our home for a good meal of elk steaks. It turned out that he was a geology student returning home for the summer. In his pack he had some dymethylglyoxime, a chemical used in testing ore for the presence of nickel. A few of our samples proved positive for nickel. This was very interesting indeed. On the almost sheer face of the mountain, above the talus slope where we had gathered our samples, were many veins of ore that we could see with binoculars from the bottom. It seemed certain that some of those veins carried nickel. Which ones? And how many? Did we have a new Sudbury? We were going to have to climb that face and take samples from each vein for analysis.

The face of the cliff had a large fault running up it at a steep angle. The fault was a narrow canyon, ten to thirty feet wide, with sheer sides. At the top it gave access to the face we needed to explore. This was the route we would have to follow to approach the veins, located at a considerable height to the right of the canyon. The face was not absolutely sheer, but broken up with many ledges. I was of the opinion that it would be feasible, though fairly dangerous, to climb these ledges by zigzagging up through them, picking our way as best we could. Even though I would have to go it alone, I decided to make the attempt the following weekend.

The year before, we had found a tremendous vein of ore on the north branch of the East Fork, across the valley from the Gail M. This was a big black vein from ten to twenty feet wide, running on the surface for twelve hundred feet. We staked it, and called it the Black Ace. We sent samples away for analysis and found it was magnetite, another ore of iron. It was worth seven dollars a ton loaded on board ship at Vancouver. No fortune to be made there!

This ore was interesting in that it was not only magnetic, but polarized as well. Hold a compass to one end of a sample and the north needle would swing to the ore. Turn the sample end for end and the south needle was attracted. If we stood on the vein with compass in hand, the needles aligned themselves with the vein, although it did not run north and south.

On a brilliant Saturday morning I drove up East Fork road as far as I could and walked up the trail to the fork of that creek. It was my full intention to climb the ledges to the veins where I expected to find the nickel ore.

At the fork I took the trail leading to the Black Ace. I'll never know why. There was no feeling of premonition, no sense of potential disaster, nothing. I was almost surprised to find myself on the wrong trail.

In half an hour I was at the lower end of the Black Ace vein, where it emerged from the overburden on an avalanche path. We had cached a tin can and a glass bottle of coffee here beside a spring. I started a brew going and sat with my back to the slope while I waited. Since I was then facing the Gail M, where I had intended to climb, I drew out my binoculars and began studying the veins and the ledges leading to them.

There came the distant clatter of falling rock, a familiar sound in the high country where weathered pinnacles are forever finding a lower level. The clatter increased to a roar, with heavy cracking sounds. This was more than just a few rocks sloughing off. The sound was coming from the direction of the Gail M, and I searched through the binoculars for the source.

Thousands of tons of rock were pouring down through the fault canyon where I had intended to climb! Near the top of the canyon, boulders half the size of a bungalow were breaking off the main face and bounding down, grinding themselves to small fragments. By the time they reached bottom they were reduced to mere bits. A huge billow of dust boiled up. If I had been near enough I would have smelled the acrid odor of sulphur.

Had I followed my original intention to climb up through the canyon I would have been caught in there with absolutely no possibility of coming out alive.

I sat in the warm sun for a long time drinking coffee and meditating. Had Someone turned my feet to the left at the fork in the trail?

In our years of prowling through the hills, mountains, and valleys of the East Kootenay, we have from time to time stumbled onto old mineral prospects. Like our own findings, none of them amounted to shucks, but it is always intriguing to speculate on the lives of the old-timers who discovered and worked these prospects and, from whatever clues they left, to study the ingenuity and hardiness displayed by these men.

One of those that stirred my imagination is on a high ridge in the Wild Horse country. George Webber, a geologist with Cominco, estimated the workings to be as much as a hundred years old. The elevation is near seven thousand feet, very near timberline here. To the south the mountain plunges steeply down to Bear Creek, far below. To the north is a sheer cliff of about five hundred feet, with a long talus slope below, and the usual alpine basin with a small lake nestling in its folds. Anderson Creek empties from this lake into the Wild Horse.

Once, when hunting goats, Bryan noticed a few shards of rock lying on the surface of this ridge, bright with the blue and green stain of copper. The ridge was covered with a thin layer of overburden. Since it was in a shallow saddle between two peaks, there was little likelihood that this was float stemming from some other location. He picked up some of the ore and noticed that some work had been done in the distant past. Several trenches had been dug, probably in an effort to reach bedrock and locate the veins from which the ore had come. The trenches had filled with soil blown in by the winds of time and were barely visible.

During the winter we had the samples assayed: 60 ounces of silver to the ton, 4.5 percent copper, 17 percent lead; definitely food for thought.

The following summer we climbed back up to take another look. It was a hard, long climb, four hours from the floor of the valley for two men in good physical condition, two hours from the nearest water. We worked out the course of several trenches and found ore along all of them. The largest piece we found was the size of a dinner plate and three inches thick.

A point of rock jutted out from the face of the cliff on the north side, and we climbed out on it so we were looking back on the vertical surface. We thought we might be able to see traces of the vein there. To our surprise, a tunnel had been driven into the face about twenty feet from the crest. It was then that we started to conjecture about the man or men who had worked the prospect, and the conditions under which they had labored.

Consider: to drive the tunnel they had to have drill steel. To sharpen the steel they had to have some kind of forge and some blacksmith tools. Since the prospect was above timberline, they probably packed in coal to fire the forge. And where did they get the coal a hundred years ago? It must have been packed in from some distant place.

Two hours from the nearest water — more by horse, since horses couldn't have come by the route we took on foot — they must have packed in water, as well as food and all necessary camp equipment. When this was done, they must have turned the horses loose to find their way back down the mountain, since there was no feed or water for them. It was a relatively small operation, so there was probably only one man, or possibly two, involved.

He or they must have clung to the almost sheer face of the cliff by ropes to get the tunnel started. From the knob of rock we were on, we could see that the tunnel drove into the face just a short distance from where they presumably intersected the vein, then turned and drifted along it.

The rock of the cliff was severely fractured and rotten. The roof of the portal had fallen in, so the entrance was at a slope, the roof material now on the floor. George

Webber, the geologist, warned us not to enter the tunnel because of the danger of noxious gas.

Did the tunnel cave in after the men abandoned it or are their bodies still in there? What is the real story? Probably it is not at all as I have visualized it; nevertheless, these thoughts are intriguing.

When we uncovered the vein in the old trenches it proved to be only three inches wide. Webber's advice was to drop the whole thing as worthless.

Fossil Basin

❖   ❖   ❖

EVEN TO GARY, WITH ALL his years of experience in the mountains, the day was memorable for several reasons. On this day he introduced his son, eleven-year-old Eric, and Eric's pal, Chad Paulson, fourteen, to the fascinating world above timberline in the Hughes Range of the Canadian Rockies.

Eric and Chad couldn't have had a better initiation. They were given the opportunity to observe a great variety of wild animals — not the beggars the road-bound tourists see along the highways, nor the poor specimens cooped up in a zoo, but animals in their natural environment doing the things they have done for untold thousands of years. As an added bonus they received a few basic lessons on the dangers of mountaineering.

The excursion was not just a hit-or-miss hike in the mountains. They had a destination in mind — the Fossil Basin. There they would receive an education in evolution that couldn't be duplicated in a classroom.

It was one o'clock on a hot August afternoon when they left Gary's jeep well below the foot of a great alpine cirque not far from Cranbrook. Twenty minutes of stiff

climbing brought them to the edge of an avalanche path
where they had a clear view of the basin.

The air here at five thousand feet (fifteen hundred
meters) was startling in its clarity. In contrast to the brown,
burned, smoggy valley at home, the basin showed a hundred
shades of color, from the darker green tones of the fir and
spruce-clad mountain shoulders to the variegated grasses
and flowers clothing the open slopes. Jagged peaks loomed
over them to the north and south, aloof and majestic. The
sheer bulk of the mountain they were on was overpowering
to the boys. The summit they were aiming for seemed
unattainable.

Hundreds of unseen folds in the surface of the basin
gave the wild animals cover in what from the road below
appeared to be wide-open space. Even as they scanned the
basin, three bighorn rams came from one of the folds and
climbed unhurriedly to a saddle leading to the next basin.
The rams stood for a few moments on the skyline, their
blocky bodies and blunt heads outlined against the blue sky.

There were countless Columbia ground squirrels
whistling and scurrying about. Annie, the expedition's little
mongrel mascot, nearly went mad trying to come to grips
with them. A short distance higher, toward the summit, a
great mule deer buck with antlers still in the velvet came out
of a thicket of shin-tangle, accompanied by two does. They
trotted up the opposite side of the watercourse Gary and the
boys were negotiating, pausing a couple of times to stare
back.

Then a large, dark coyote showed himself on a
rimrock above them on the left. He began barking at them,
not the usual falsetto yapping of his kind, but a deep bay
almost resembling a wolf's call. Gary at once knew there
was something strange in the animal's behavior. He looked

in the opposite direction and saw another, smaller coyote high on that side of the defile.

This second animal was no doubt the mother of a litter; the first one, the father, was attempting to decoy these dangerous interlopers away from his little family. When Gary and the boys moved toward him he would be quiet and hide. When they moved toward the female and family he would show himself, barking. Once, when the group continued moving on toward his wards, he actually came a long way down the slope, barking all the way. It showed the boys how some species of animals lived up to their family responsibilities, even at the risk of death.

The travelers stopped to eat their lunch at the last water they would find in the basin. As they sat there in the bright sunlight a golden eagle came swooping at great speed over the rim. He dipped sharply in an effort to grasp a gopher in his talons and, failing, soared off over another summit out of sight. Almost immediately another eagle, surely the first one's mate, ripped in over the rim a short distance away, using the same tactics. It, too, failed, and for half an hour Gary and the boys watched as the eagles made pass after pass all in vain. Of the gophers Gary said, "The dumb ones are all dead."

After more steep but open climbing up a grassy slope, the party reached the high saddle. The last few steps to the top gradually revealed the scene to the east. It was the first time the boys had viewed the mountains from a like height, and they were excited over the vista that unfolded before them. As far as they could see stood peak after peak; hundreds, no, thousands of them. And on each mountain there were several cirques similar to the one they had just surmounted. In nearly every one of the hundreds of folds and valleys between the peaks ran a small stream, unseen of course from their present viewpoint. On some of the peaks they could see glaciers that fed the streams. Some of the peaks were lower than the one on which they stood, and many towered far higher. The ones nearer at hand stood out hard and clear, in the middle distance they faded into a faint blue haze, and farther off still they were indistinct.

The boys knew enough about local geography to understand that far beyond their range of vision lay the prairies of Alberta. For perhaps the first time they had a true conception of the vastness of the Rocky Mountains.

The thought never occurred to them as they stood there, but when they grew older they would think of the wildlife they saw on this day, on this one mountain, and they would come to realize what a wealth of life existed in this vast area they were viewing. Their whole lifetimes could be spent exploring the expanse before them, and they would never see it all. Disneyland? Who needs Disneyland?

The basin now confronting them was north-facing, smaller but much more rugged than the one they had surmounted. A green jewel of a lake nestled in the bottom. Here they had a choice of routes. They could make their way easily to the bottom, where they faced a stiff climb up the opposite slope, or they could take a difficult, shorter, and more dangerous way across a huge, dark cliff to the right. The second choice was appealing, for it would mean holding their present elevation, eliminating the need to climb the opposite slope.

They chose a broad ledge for the attack on the cliff, but the ledge soon petered out until it was barely the width of a human foot. There was also an overhang on the upper side. Tantalizingly near, the ledge again widened with easy going to a vast, steep field of snow, residue of last winter's fall.

The situation was not all that dangerous, with a wider ledge six meters below, but a sliding fall to it would at least result in bruises and contusions. Gary demonstrated how, by facing the overhanging rock and pressing their hands against it, it was possible to shuffle crabwise along the ledge. If the pressure on the hands neared zero it was time to back off, because the point of balance was near. He also pointed out that the exuberant dog, by attempting to press by them, could force them off the ledge.

He sent Annie across first, then shied a few rocks in her direction to discourage her. She slunk out onto the snow and sat there dejectedly while first Gary, then Chad, and finally Eric crossed safely. Thus the boys had their first lesson in free climbing in the rocks.

Having gained the snow, Gary found the surface to be loose crystals, hard-packed underneath. The footing was good, but a fall would result in a terrifyingly fast slide to the frowning black rocks fifty meters below.

Annie gave them a first-class demonstration. They had reached a very steep section when she sat down and promptly began to slide. In seconds she was fairly flying down the mountain, her front feet braced, ears flapping behind, snow crystals spraying like the rooster tail of a fast boat.

The boys were frightened. They thought the dog would be killed when she hit the rocks. But the snow leveled off a bit, and down near the bottom where it wasn't so deep, the crystals turned to slush with the comparative warmth of the earth underneath. Annie slid to a spectacular stop.

Far from being frightened, she had found a great new game. She scampered back up to them, turned around and, lowering to her elbows, took off again. They watched in amusement as she repeated the performance several times. Each time she returned to them she gamboled about in great glee before embarking again down the slide.

Finally in her gamboling she hit Chad behind the knees, and in a heartbeat he was sliding down the snow on his back straight toward the jagged black rocks. But he too hit the slush in a cloud of flying spray and regained his feet just short of disaster.

They were now near the 7,000-foot level, well above timberline, and another small, gloomy basin stretched above them. This was Fossil Basin.

The snowfield was behind them. Unseen pikas were crying plaintively from a rock slide to one side. Gary showed the boys how they gathered grass for their winter's food, drying it on the rocks when the weather was fair and taking it into shelter when rain threatened. Efficient little harvesters!

Away below them they heard the whistling of a colony of marmots. Like the pikas, they kept well hidden, but after studying the rocks for a long time the adventurers spotted a big fat one taking the sun on top of a boulder. A minute later they saw a pika scamper across the slide next to them and huddle near the entrance to his burrow.

It was just a short climb to the scree below the cliffs of the basin. Away up in the cliffs stood a goat, white against the dark background, defying gravity with all four hooves bunched on a small pinnacle with a hundred meters of open air beneath him. A second goat browsed on a small ledge near the first. Then a patch of snow just below those two suddenly came alive. Eighteen goats moved off the snow and the whole herd climbed the vertical wall as only goats can do, disappearing finally over the peak. The boys were astounded at the reckless performance.

Fossils! Hundreds of them lay in the scree. Dozens

more showed on the surface of the solid rock. Gary cautioned the boys that they must not destroy the ones in place by hammering them. They scampered here and there picking up samples from the ground. They were allowed to take a very few home with them, and they selected, discarded, and selected again until they were weary. The fossils were mainly sponges and other acquatic growth, with some shellfish here and there. Chad made the find of the day, a section of backbone with ribs attached, obviously of a vertebrate, probably a reptile. Here, at an elevation of 7,500 feet (about 2,300 meters) was what had once been the floor of an ocean.

The excitement was over for the day. It remained to make their way back to the jeep, and the afternoon was nearly spent. It was seven o'clock before they reached the vehicle, weary and hungry.

The next day I asked Eric, my grandson, how he had enjoyed the day. With typical eleven-year-old nonchalance, he answered, "OK, I guess."

"How do you feel?"

He rubbed his thighs. "A little stiff."

"Would you like to go again?"

The answer came quickly. "Oh, yeah!"

III

❖　❖　❖

THE HUNT

The .30-.30 Winchester

❖   ❖   ❖

THE FIRST RIFLE I OWNED was a boy-size .22-caliber
Cooey Canuck. Some friend of the family gave it to me, but
because I was only about five years old the firing pin had
been removed. The barrel was rusted out and badly pitted,
but it served admirably as a toy gun for a young lad whose
father and older brothers were keen hunters.

A couple of years after I had come into possession of
it we moved to another house in Wardner where Pa built a
two-car garage. We owned only one vehicle, but I suppose
he had an eye to the future. In any case he built half of it
into a workshop with a bench, a vise, a small forge, and a
scattering of the more common tools, such as pliers, files,
and punches. I was quite interested in the work that went on
in there, and I even took on a few small projects of my own.

Then came a brilliant idea. Why not make and
install a new firing pin in the old Cooey? I took a piece of
stiff wire, cut it off to what seemed the proper length, filed
it down to fit the firing pin hole, and after many attempts
succeeded in getting the gun to fire once in maybe ten tries.

My brothers had a .22, and there was always a box
or two of cartridges around the house. It was no problem

snitching a few from time to time and sneaking down to the
brushy hillside near the cemetery for a little target practice.
I had to be careful not to take too many cartridges for fear
of being discovered. In any case the rifle was inaccurate; the
bullets came out of the barrel end over end in the so-called
keyhole effect. My slingshot was much more accurate and
didn't misfire, so I abandoned the old .22. What became of
it I can't recall.

About this time I came down with chicken pox and
was confined to bed for a week or so. I wasn't very sick and
I still couldn't read very well, so time dragged. I suppose I
made impossible demands on my mother's time. One evening Pa brought me his Winchester to play with in bed.

From time to time he would look in on me, offering
instruction. I had learned with the Cooey how to align the
sights, but Pa improved on that simple procedure. "Don't
tip the gun like that. Keep the sights right on top. Don't yank
the trigger — pull it slow. See how the sights move off the
target when you yank it?"

If I laid the rifle down for even a moment, I had to
open the action when I picked it up again to make sure it
was unloaded. He pinned the picture of a whitetail buck on
the wall. "Always aim behind the shoulder unless he's awful
close, then aim for the neck. Don't try to shoot him in the
head. The target is too small, and there's a chance you might
hit him in the nose or jaw. Aim for the neck."

By the time I was back in school I had a good
working knowledge of the rifle and its action. I knew how
to align the sights and squeeze off a shot. I had spent hours
dry-firing. A good basic education, considering my age.

I didn't realize then how many pleasurable hours I
would spend with that rifle, nor what it would eventually
come to mean to me.

Our parents had come from Sweden to Canada in 1909. A year later they came to the East Kootenay Valley, and here Pa discovered that the hills were loaded with whitetail deer. He sent to Eaton's for a Marlin .30-.30, but the sights were canted off to one side. In 1916 he disposed of it and ordered a Winchester replacement. In due time he received a Model 94, the famous carbine of the West. He paid the grand sum of nineteen dollars and fifty cents for it. It had a cedar stock and fore end instead of the usual walnut, and had probably been made for a special promotional sale by Eaton's.

The serial number was 551752, and a check with Winchester many years later revealed that it had been made sometime between 1911 and 1916, probably about 1914.

Pa's success with the new rifle was extraordinary. Being a generous person, he often lent it to other hunters in Wardner, and gradually it developed a reputation as "the rifle that couldn't miss." Emil Shellborn, now living in Jaffray, remembers it well, and on occasion borrowed it himself. Many others who owned rifles but had suffered a run of bad luck borrowed it too, and almost invariably came home with their bucks.

When I was about twelve, being the brat that I was, I had taken to swiping the rifle and smuggling it out to the hills. Tuckahiro (Charlie) Miyasaki, my very best friend, and I used to go on long hunts, always with the intention of killing a deer, but somehow we never succeeded. I couldn't shoot at targets because the missing cartridges would have been noticed at once. Pa rarely had more than one box on hand, and since he was very sparing of ammunition the box was usually near empty. Even a cartridge or two out of a total of ten or so would have given me away. I don't know what Charlie and I would have done had we killed a deer. I guess we thought we would worry about that when the time came. Anyway, punishment was never severe. Pa would have probably just smiled inside his mouth while telling me never to do it again.

I was fifteen before I killed my first deer up on Pickering Hill. It was January, the season was closed, and I had no license. My partner for the day was Bayard Iverson, schoolteacher and scoutmaster. Obviously we were living in a quite free society, at least as far as hunting was concerned.

The next fall I took two goats in one day with the Winchester. I took my first elk with it, too, and over the years several black bears. One evening in 1947 I killed a "black" bear that had an odd sandy color. His underfur was tinted an odd pale orange. A man was in the area collecting small rodents for the Peabody Museum at Yale, and he bought the hide from me for five dollars. I often wonder whether that hide is still in the museum collection.

I recall a couple of incidents when the "rifle that couldn't miss" lived up to its reputation. Sonny Johnston once borrowed it when we were on a hunting expedition in the Devil's Fryingpan above Torrent. There were mule deer by the hundreds there, and Sonny took a shot at a big buck at unbelievable range. A knowledgeable hunter would never have attempted the shot. The deer didn't even run. He walked about fifty yards and piled up. When we skinned the deer we found that the bullet had gone up through the brisket and embedded itself in the heart. It had ricocheted off the ground to do its work.

Another time Elwood Goodwin, Alta's brother, killed his first goat up on Boulder Creek near Wilmer. On our way off the mountain with the goat on our packboards, we came out on the edge of a horseshoe-shaped rimrock overlooking a rocky basin. Away down in the bottom a big billy was browsing on the brush. We were directly above him. Just to see what his reaction would be, we tipped a big boulder over the edge of the cliff. It bounded down, loosening several more as it plunged toward the billy. He was far, far down below what had now developed into a handsome rockslide, but he well knew the danger from falling rocks.

He began to run for the shelter of a steep little ridge. Intending to spur him to even greater effort, I fired a shot high over his back. I had no intention of hitting the animal. It should have been impossible; I should have known better. The bullet hit him right behind the shoulder, and we watched in consternation as he slowed and finally fell.

The rifle was my father's proudest possession. For the last few years of his life he was an invalid. Depression times being what they were, I had no rifle of my own, so it was natural that I should use his. Before he died, he gave me the gun with the understanding that I would never, never sell it. I carried it for perhaps thousands of miles on my shoulder over those Depression years, until it became as much a part of me as my clothing. Money was scarce and I was rationed a box of twenty cartridges per month. I recall that a box of twenty cost one dollar and sixty-five cents, and that amount supplied us with most of our meat requirements. Not bad, even in those times.

Eventually old age took its toll on the rifle, even as it does on us all. The soft cedar stock and fore end became worn, scratched and gouged in a hundred places. The tang holding the stock to the action became loose. Sonny Johnston had come by an old .32 Special Model 96 Winchester that had the same peculiarity as my old Cooey Canuck — the bullets tumbled end over end as they came from the muzzle. Sonny decided to trade it for a pair of homemade goat-hide chaps. Before he made the deal we switched stocks on the two rifles. Sonny's deal turned out a bit funny. We could always tell where Sonny rode wearing those chaps by the clumps of white wool clinging to the bushes.

When we attended Pa's funeral I wasn't happy with the eulogy delivered by the minister. The next day I took the old rifle that Pa had loved so well and went for a long, long walk in the hills. I didn't take any ammunition. I walked for miles thinking back on Pa's life and trying in my own humble way to say goodbye.

Eventually I bought a new Husqvarna .270, a rifle that I believed then, and still do, is the optimum rifle for our needs in this part of the world. The old .30-.30 was by now so worn in the action that I feared it was no longer safe to use, so I put it into semi-retirement. Our boys used it sparingly until they bought rifles of their own, and after that I used it only once a year for old-time's sake. Each fall for several more years I made a point of taking one deer with it, but finally and reluctantly I decided that it should be put aside before someone got hurt. I removed the firing pin.

One of the hardest decisions of my life was which one of our sons should inherit Pa's Winchester. I finally decided that, since I was the youngest of our family and had inherited it from Pa, I should pass it on to our youngest. I gave it to Ray on the understanding that it should never, never be sold, and that it should have a place of honor among his possessions.

Perhaps the story of how I acquired and lost my .270 Husqvarna is worth the telling. I was mustered out of the Rocky Mountain Rangers in 1945, and with our discharge we were given the opportunity to buy surplus First World War U.S. Army Enfield rifles for the sum of five dollars each. I bought one that still had the factory grease in the barrel. Of course it had the military stock with wood right to the muzzle, and was a heavy, clumsy contraption. Oscar had taken up re-stocking rifles as a hobby, and he built me a beautiful walnut stock to my own specifications at no cost to me. I cut an inch and a half off the end of the barrel, crowned it, altered the trigger-pull, and ended up with a fine, dependable sporting rifle.

Alta's brother Elwood had returned from overseas, where he had liberated two pairs of Zeiss 6x30 binoculars. He gave me one pair. I wasn't doing much mountain hunting at that time, and didn't have much use for the binoculars. I traded them straight across to the R and M Sports Shop in Cranbrook for a four-power Weaver scope and mounts. Now I had a rifle-scope combination beyond my fondest dreams.

A friend of mine fell in love with the rifle and offered to buy it. I didn't want to part with it, so put a price on it that I thought he was sure to refuse. To my consternation he took me up on it, and paid me one hundred and twenty dollars.

Just at that time, 1949, the R and M Sports Shop received its first postwar shipment of European rifles, Swedish Husqvarnas in .30-.06 and .270 calibers. One of the .270s caught my eye. It was stocked with a fine piece of European walnut with a tawny cast. I bought it, with a Lyman aperture sight and a box of shells, for one hundred and seventeen dollars. Here I had what I considered to be the finest rifle I could wish for, and certainly it met my every expectation over the next thirty years. The one drawback was that I had parted with the scope sight on the rifle I sold. Alta and Bryan corrected that by giving me a six-power Weaver scope for my birthday.

As I said, I carried that rifle for thirty years, until it was stolen one dark night in 1980. Oscar had by now developed his stock-making hobby into a full-fledged gunsmithing business, and just prior to the theft had reblued the rifle for me. Aside from a few minor scratches on the stock, the rifle was in perfect condition. My heart was all but broken.

Luckily the loss was covered with insurance, and the insurance company paid me three hundred and eighty dollars, by then the replacement cost of the rifle-scope combination.

So, on an initial outlay of five dollars, I made a total profit of three hundred and seventy-eight dollars, and I had used the Husqvarna for thirty years!

The Trophy Hunter

❖ ❖ ❖

TROPHY HUNTERS CAN BE divided into two groups. There are those who have not hunted much and so have not killed a great number of game animals. To them nearly any legal animal is a "trophy." Even a spike elk, say, if they have never seen one before, is a pretty imposing animal. Or a yearling grizzly. It's important to them to be able to return home and say they killed a grizzly, elk, or whatever, and from there embellish the adventure as they see fit.

The other group of people have killed a fair number of animals and then resolved to take only outstanding game. To them the greatest importance is bagging a rare animal, and of course to shoot an animal with an outstanding head is the most common ambition. I consider these latter to be the true "trophy hunters."

A lot of people have very strong feelings about the trophy hunter on the grounds that nourishing meat is often left behind and therefore wasted. It often happens that, to collect a trophy, the hunter must travel into remote country, often on foot, with the result that when he does make a kill it is impossible to carry the meat out.

Then there are the nonresident hunters who have

come perhaps halfway around the world to hunt in our little corner. Their problems of taking the perishable goodies home are formidable, indeed.

Here let me say that I am not a trophy hunter myself. I am a meat hunter, one of those who grew up during a time when wild meat was an important part of our economy. We shunned the larger animals because they were not so palatable. I must admit, however, that I have always kept an eye out for a truly unusual animal, and if one should cross my path I would probably take him. I have never killed a grizzly, although I have had many opportunities and many of my clients have taken them thanks to my efforts. The idea of eating a grizzly is not very appealing, and a rug on the floor is just something to be trampled into a travesty of the animal from which it came. The proper place for a bear hide is on a wall, but there are not many walls in the average home big enough to display a truly large grizzly hide.

I have had occasion to guide a few trophy hunters and I have seen a lot of meat left in the hills. Many people would regard that meat as wasted. Wasted? Not so.

Many of us in our ignorance believe that the human animal is the only one in creation who has the right to benefit from the death of our wild animals. This is arrogant thinking. There are others besides ourselves who benefit from a good feed of protein, and they are every bit as entitled to it as we are. These fall into two groups: the predators and the scavengers.

In our past society the scavengers were classed very low in the pecking order. Still, our attitudes are changing. We now admit that in the class of scavengers there are some noble animals, after all. The grizzly bear and the bald eagle are a couple. Only a generation ago they were being killed on sight as "varmints."

To those of us fortunate enough to have watched a pair of grizzly cubs at their roly-poly play, with mother nearby tearing a rockslide apart in pursuit of a scant mouthful of prey, or to have seen an eagle soar effortlessly past as we clung with laboring lungs to the side of a steep mountain, the thought must come that we are not so great in the scheme of things as we would like to believe. Can we reason that any food these creatures consume is wasted? We could go down a long, long list of these scavengers, all the way to the worms in the ground, but one thing is clear: Mother Nature never sees anything "wasted." Within minutes or at most a few hours after a trophy has been skinned and abandoned, the scavengers arrive. Everything edible is eaten. The few bones that are left eventually decompose and enter the soil. And who knows, perhaps a seedling tree will take root there in the enriched soil where the animal fell, and grow a bit taller and straighter than those surrounding it. If the animal were not killed by human hands, it would be only a matter of time before it died of natural causes. The end result would be the same.

Take Frank Manners, the "Man from Missouri" with whom I had the great good fortune to be associated. He had come to hunt for bighorn sheep in the Wild Horse area, back in the fifties. Within a couple of hours of making camp he had killed a ram on the mountain slope just above the tents.

It was not a large animal, although to him it was a "trophy," and he resolved to come back the next year for a full-curl ram. He came back for fourteen consecutive years before he realized his ambition. In that time he killed only one sick old nanny goat, in an act of compassion, and a mule deer destined to feed a party of inept hunters camped on the other side of the mountain, who were all but starving for want of fresh meat.

His lack of success was not due to a scarcity of sheep, for he had passed up any number of common specimens, but he was determined to shoot nothing but an outstanding specimen. Eventually he was successful. And did we feel guilty because we left most of the meat in that remote basin where the ram fell? Not at all.

From that little yarn we can deduce that the dedicated trophy hunter kills far less game than the hunters who fill their licenses, whether they are the other group of trophy hunters or the meat hunters. Furthermore, any hunter who has bought licenses and tags, spent thousands of dollars on equipment, transportation, and services, and lived up to all the regulations pertaining to the hunt has the right to do with his animal as he chooses. If he lets the carcass lie and then returns home to buy a beef for his freezer, the whole show is probably good for our ailing economy. It is good for the bear, the coyote and wolverine, for the eagle, the crow, the raven, and the magpie.

This subject is stirring up much controversy. I can't say mine is the only correct view. It's just the way I see it.

How to Get Unlost

❖ ❖ ❖

THE ELK TRACKS WERE UNDOUBTEDLY fresh. They had been imprinted in the couple of inches of snow only a few minutes before I came by. It was snowing fairly hard and had been for an hour or so, but the black clods turned up by the elk's hooves had just a light dusting of the white crystals. It was late in the afternoon and the tracks were going in my direction, so I followed them with a sharp eye peeled ahead. If the elk paused to feed, as they very well might considering the time of day, I would most likely come up with them.

This was strange country to me. I had often hunted the big ridge to my left with success, but on this day I had decided to circle the ridge at a much lower level to see what the country was like on the long northern slope. I had been disappointed. Nearly the whole day I had been thrashing through a horrendous thicket of second-growth fir and larch. But now my built-in computer told me I would soon break out into more open country, country I knew well.

Here the big ridge was fairly heavily wooded with a mixture of mature pine, larch, and fir, with occasional clearings up the slope. In one of these, just about at the limit of my vision through the falling snow, another herd of about ten or twelve elk was coming down from the ridge to intercept my line of travel. I sank down on one knee, pretending to be a stump, and waited. . . .

They were only a hundred yards away when an old cow spotted me and stopped to consider that queer object below. I picked out a four-point bull and touched the trigger. Instantly the herd broke for the timber, and for a moment the bull was lost in the confusion. Then he lagged behind and finally tumbled down in a flurry of snow.

The snow kept falling as I dressed and quartered the animal. I laid the quarters out to cool on a couple of convenient poles, tossed the head and antlers into an old burned-out stump hole, then took stock of the situation. Although I had my packboard with me I didn't want to load a quarter on my back and stumble around trying to find an easy way to my truck. It seemed better to leave the whole thing while I scouted my way out. There would be plenty of time on the following day to recover the meat.

I had gone quite a distance before I came to the bottom of a big, wide draw flanking the ridge. Dead ahead was a series of steep, broken hills. This wasn't going to be easy.

I heard a sawmill start up way off to the west. I knew that country well, and I couldn't for the life of me understand what a mill was doing over there. It had been logged off not too long before. There had been a mill running earlier in the day off to the north, and gradually it dawned on me — I was about ninety degrees off in my reckoning.

If I had continued in the direction I was going, I would have found myself spending the night huddled beside a fire in some awesomely rugged country. Because the mill had started up when it did, with only a few minutes left in the normal working day, I had become aware of my error.

And it simplified things considerably. A shift of ninety degrees sent me happily down the wide draw, which was not only open but all downhill! Soon I came to country I knew, and a few minutes later was tapping the thermos in my truck. The snow had stopped falling, and it would be easy to follow my tracks in the morning.

The next morning, however, I awoke to find a good foot of new snow on the ground. Up where the elk lay there would be more. Backtracking would be impossible. As I munched my bacon and eggs another disturbing thought came to me. Had I become disoriented before I shot the elk, or after? That was going to make a big difference in trying to find my way back. Another thing: the quarters were lying flat on the little poles and I had put the antlers into the stump hole. Nothing would be sticking up to catch my eye. With a foot or more of virgin snow hiding the elk even from the birds, it was more likely I would never find it.

Maybe it came from living right, or maybe it was just dumb luck (the latter seems more likely), but I climbed the ridge to what seemed to be the right elevation and started to circle it at that height. It was easier to look for the big opening where I had made the kill than to look for one comparatively small elk. I walked right into the clearing, and then finding the carcass was easy. The trip out the previous evening had showed me that it was downhill nearly all the way to the truck. I loaded one quarter on my packboard, tied a rope to another, and, packing one and dragging the other, after a couple of sweaty hours I was back having lunch in the truck. The second trip was easier over a broken trail.

This was the nearest I have ever come to being lost, but I have always considered the possibility. Even if I had spent the night out I would have been in no great danger. Of course the sensible thing to do in that event would be to build a fire and wait to be rescued. I'm an impatient man, however, and I don't believe I could sit around for a couple of days waiting. And a couple of days without water (and cigarettes?) would drive nearly anyone back onto his feet.

In mountainous country such as ours, where the watersheds are precipitous and therefore relatively short, there is one sure, simple solution to being lost. All you have to do is *walk downhill*. Soon you'll come to water. Follow the water down and you'll come to human habitation. It may take a day or two, even three or four. You may get hungry, but you won't die of thirst. One thing is certain: it does beat walking in circles.

This ploy will not work everywhere, of course. For instance, if you were lost up near the tree line in the north and followed these instructions, you could walk for a year or more only to find yourself standing on the shore of the Arctic Ocean. But in parts of the country similar to ours — steep country with logging or mining roads up nearly every creek — it is sure-fire.

I am continually amazed at the reports of people who have become lost in our area, some of them to spend days in the wilderness, some never to be heard of again. In most of these cases their problem should have been solved easily. No need to know which is north, south, east, or west. All they had to do was walk downhill.

An article appeared in one of our outdoor magazines recently, relating how a seventeen-year-old youth, Greg Martin of Creston, B.C., had become disoriented while hunting on Kid Creek, fifteen miles northeast of Creston. He spent a horrendous night in the mountains and was lucky to be found alive. I have not walked that area, but a quick glance at a topographical map shows that he was lost within a few miles of a logging road. All he needed to do, once he was sure he was disoriented, was to walk downhill, and he would have been standing on the road up which he had driven in the morning. Two or three hours at the most, and his ordeal would have been over. Even if there had been no road in that watershed, following Kid Creek down would have brought him to Highway 3 in just a few hours. Instead, he walked uphill and crossed into another watershed.

In my own case, the day I killed the elk, I would not have stayed out longer than overnight. If I had determined I was disoriented, all I would have had to do is walk downhill, and in less than an hour I would have been in the bottom of the valley. Following the water down, I would have come to my truck in less than another hour.

The lesson is easy to remember. *Walk downhill.*

Sasquatch

❖   ❖   ❖

STEVENSON, Washington (Associated Press), April 1984 — Bigfoot, the apelike creature that legend says roams the forests of the Pacific Northwest, is now the sole creature on the endangered species list of Skamania County.

The three commissioners of the largely rural south Washington county voted Monday to make it a misdemeanor to kill a Bigfoot in the county.

Killing a Bigfoot — or Sasquatch, as the animal is also known — in Skamania County will be a crime punishable by up to one year in jail and a $5,000 fine under an ordinance passed unanimously by the three commissioners.

The commissioners did not try to prove or disprove Bigfoot's existence, but they listened as several people testified about their own experiences with the legendary beast.

The ordinance was sparked by reports that a group led by Mark E. Keller of Arcata, California, plans to mount a hunt in an undisclosed location this spring to prove the creatures exist.

The thought of hunters stalking Bigfoot with high-powered rifles in a part of Skamania County frequented by campers and hikers worried county prosecutor Robert Leick and Rou Craft, editor emeritus of the Skamania County Pioneer *newspaper.*

If anyone kills a Bigfoot in Skamania County, Leick — who doubles as county coroner — is empowered to examine the remains. If he determines the creature is humanoid, the killer could be charged with murder.

Datus Perry of Carson said he had seen giant apes in Skamania County and in California, but declined to reveal specific locations for fear someone might go there and stalk the creatures.

Perry, 72, a retired diesel engineer, imitated the high-pitched, whistling call he said the creatures make.

He said the fine hair on their faces is "like black velvet," and they have powerful shoulders, coarse body hair and do not smell bad, contrary to some other reports.

ON A FINE, CLEAR DAY IN June 1963, a friend of mine, who doesn't want to be identified, was walking up a logging road that winds along the bank of Cedar Creek. A mile behind him his logging truck had broken down, and he was faced with a long walk out to the logging camp where he could get help. The crew of men who had loaded his logging truck had passed him on their way to camp in their faster crew truck, so he was alone.

The road ran close to the roaring mountain stream, the noise of the turbulent waters effectively muffling the clump of his caulked boots. At one point the creek and road bent together, revealing a boulder-strewn slide dead ahead of my friend. He saw a dark, furry creature amongst the rocks of the slide. It was quite large, and at first he took it to be a bear. There were a lot of grizzlies in the area, and as a matter of caution he paused to take a reading of the situation.

In about a minute the animal moved out into a comparatively clear space, and my friend realized with a shock that he was looking at Sasquatch, British Columbia's legendary half-man, half-beast creature. Like most people, he had heard and read many stories of Sasquatch, but had taken it all with a grain of salt. Here was proof!

The Sasquatch moved slowly amongst the rocks, evidently feeding on berries. It moved in an upright position, walking on its hind feet. In its rather hunched posture it stood about five feet high. My friend estimated its weight at three to four hundred pounds. The body was covered with sparse brown hair; the hands, resembling human hands, hung nearly to the ground. The man became acutely aware that the sun was sinking rapidly behind the mountain range, that he was alone and unarmed, and that the Sasquatch was between him and the camp. He thought of returning to his truck and barricading himself in the cab, but as it turned out he had no cause to fear.

In a few minutes the Sasquatch, possibly sensing another presence, turned and stared directly at the man, who saw clearly the open mouth with square white teeth. In another second the creature set off up the rockslide, traveling in great leaping bounds, still upright on its hind feet. It disappeared in some brush at the foot of a cliff five hundred yards up the mountain.

❖   ❖   ❖

Another very good friend of mine, whom I believe to be a person of great integrity, once asked cautiously whether I believed there really was such a creature as Sasquatch. I regaled him with my own story, which I will relate shortly. He was greatly relieved at my response. He, too, had seen not one, but two of the creatures, and had wanted to talk with someone about his experience, but he, too, was fearful of ridicule. Since I was receptive, he told me the following account:

He and a companion were driving from a point in Saskatchewan to the Okanagan District in British Columbia. My friend was at the wheel. At two in the morning, they reached the junction of the Kimberley Highway and the Fort Steele Highway, just east of the Cranbrook city limits. As they came around the sharp curve at the junction two furry, dark creatures came up the bank from the sewage lagoons and crossed the road right in front of the car. They were so close that my friend had to apply his brakes to avoid hitting one of them, even though the car was traveling slowly.

His description of the creatures was uncannily like the one given by my logger friend, except that he estimated the weight at around two hundred pounds. In addition, he gave a demonstration of the animal's posture and gait, and his performance was most convincing.

❖   ❖   ❖

One fine fall morning three of us were looking through binoculars at the basin west of Cooper Lake. Cooper Lake is the headwater of the Moyie River, about twenty miles west of Cranbrook as the crow flies, somewhat farther if the crow is walking. The sun had just risen behind us and visibility was nearly perfect, the fall air still and crystal clear. We were roughly a mile from the far end of the basin, quite a long way to be glassing, but I had a good pair of 10x50 Bushnell binoculars mounted on a low, light-weight tripod. As a big-game guide I packed everything on my back. To cut down weight I opted for the big glasses instead of the usual combination of smaller binoculars and a spotting scope. Admittedly there were drawbacks to the single instrument, but it was a good compromise. The fall before, from this same spot, I had spotted a nice, big mule-deer buck high up in the basin, and my hunters had collected him after a good stalk.

While I studied the basin segment by segment, my hunters of the day sat behind me with their own glasses. It was doubtful that they could have seen much in the way of game, but they were certainly enjoying the scenery with its vivid colors of the fall season. The lake lay between us and the basin with just a fine ripple on its surface. Here and there an occasional trout rose, breakfasting on the few surface flies not yet dormant.

After a few minutes I spotted a creature standing upright atop a small rock bluff perhaps ten feet high. It was a furry creature, and since it stood poised on its hind feet, I concluded it was a bear. It blended into the background so well that it was hard for me to make out much detail. It was big enough to make a respectable trophy, and I was about to speak out when the animal leaped from the bluff. Two things told me immediately that it was not a bear. *It jumped from its hind feet and landed upright on its hind feet.*

Just below the animal and to its right was a thicket of alders. Before I could recover from my surprise it had disappeared. I feel strongly that it had seen us at the edge of the lake in spite of the distance, and had leaped toward the nearest cover. There is really no other explanation why it should have jumped from the bluff. My first reaction was to tell the hunters that I had seen a Sasquatch. What else could it be? But a good guide has to be a bit of a psychologist, too. My hunters were strangers to me, as I was to them. The impressions we gave each other on this first day of the hunt were going to affect our relationship to a marked degree. I could imagine their reaction if I told them I had seen a Sasquatch. Forefingers drawing circles in the air beside their heads, that's what. And even for me, the whole thing required careful consideration.

To this day I don't know for certain what it was. I've been a keen observer of nature for many years, and I pride myself on my ability to interpret my observations accurately. There is no doubt in my mind that the creature actually jumped off the rock from its hind feet and landed on its hind feet. Bears don't do that. What could it be, other than a Sasquatch?

Grizzly at the Top of
the World

❖   ❖   ❖

THE GRIZZLY HAD COME UP the long game trail from
Lussier Creek in the dark hours of the morning. He stood
now in the high, bare saddle above the alpine plateau of the
Top of the World, warming his old bones in the rays of the
rising sun.

He was far past his prime. His chocolate coat was
short and sparse, and he was thin for a bear in the fall of the
year. One lower tusk was broken off short; his claws were
worn and blunt; a rear molar had a deep cavity and ached
incessantly. Matter in his eyes rendered him almost blind,
so he didn't see the hoarfrost on the grasses of the big
meadow far below. It was doubtful that he would see
another spring, and in fact, this was to be his last day.

To his left rose the imposing bulk of Sugar Loaf
Peak; to the right the ridge swept up to a lesser rounded
knob. He pawed irritably at the side of his aching face, then
paused and listened attentively to the quarreling of a flock
of Clark's nutcrackers below. Normally these birds traveled
in small family groups. This larger congregation told the
bear they had found something of interest, and it would be
worthwhile to investigate.

He moved a few feet down the eastern slope, nose raised, head swinging slightly as he searched the early breeze. A current of air brought him the message he was seeking, an odor he knew well. Somewhere down there lay a dead animal.

Unhurriedly he padded down the mountain, following the sound of the noisy birds. A hundred yards from the summit he found the animal — a dead mule deer. The ground was fairly open, with just a scattering of twisted, stunted spruce and balsam. The birds flew off the carcass at his approach and scolded raucously from the nearest trees.

He liked privacy while he fed, so after nosing the deer for a minute he seized a ham in his jaws and attempted to drag the carcass farther down the mountain, into the shelter of the bigger timber below. But the deer was hung up on one of the spruces. Impatiently the grizzly bunched his haunches and tugged powerfully in rapid sequence.

Shallow-rooted in thin soil, the spruce gave way. Finally the bear dragged both tree and deer down into the heavier timber a couple of hundred yards below. Deep in the timber he found a small glade. For an hour he fed leisurely. Finally replete, he set about burying the remains. With his stubby claws he tore up grass and soil, pawing and rooting the debris over the cache. A windfall six inches in diameter interfered with his work. Impatiently he hooked one huge paw over it, and with a tremendous bunching of his shoulders broke it off cleanly. The crash of the breaking wood echoed back from Sugar Loaf Peak. Startled birds rose from the treetops above him, then settled down again. They were much quieter now.

The bear nosed over the heap of debris to satisfy himself that he had done an adequate job. Then, from up near where he had found the deer, came the tinkle of moving shale. He stopped and raised his nose to the thermal breeze that still flowed fitfully down the mountain. He didn't like the scent that came to him. Vaguely uneasy, and growing angry at this intrusion, he crouched down in the shadow of his cache and waited tensely.

The year was 1947. I had hired out to Jim White at Fort Steele, British Columbia, as a guide. Our four hunters for the thirty-day trip were two father-and-son teams, of whom my personal charge was Don Warren, Jr. They were all from the San Francisco area.

Don junior and I were the same age, twenty-nine, but while I was in very good physical shape, Don had a stiff knee, the result of a college football injury. When I first met him I had misgivings. How would he fare on the hunt, considering that we would have to do much hard climbing on foot in the rugged mountains of East Kootenay's Hughes Range? Handicapped as he was, I was afraid that much of our time would be spent within sight of camp.

I needn't have worried. For sheer guts Don junior surpassed anybody I ever knew, before or since. The first day, from our initial camp at Fish Lake, we climbed laboriously to a high basin above timberline. There Don killed a good goat, drawing first blood for the party. The only concession we made to Don's infirmity was that I carried his rifle for him.

Don was not an experienced hunter; neither was he very familiar with his rifle. That fact was made clear when he missed the finishing shot at his goat from forty feet. It was to surface again later with almost disastrous results when we faced an angry grizzly at close range.

Don senior, on the other hand, had spent his boy-
hood on a farm in the Midwest, and with the rifle he was
deadly. Jim White was his guide, and with all his years of
experience, he maintained that Don senior was the best
game shot he had ever seen. We had reason to be thankful
for that when the chips were down.

These were the days of plentiful game and consequently liberal bag limits. The East Kootenay District
offered a diversity of big game: bighorn sheep, goats, two
species of deer, grizzly and black bears, moose, elk, caribou
on the west slope of the valley, and of course the predators
— cougar, coyote, wolverine.

Fish Lake was essentially a goat camp. But during
our stay there, a wandering moose fell on the meadow at the
lake's edge, an early-morning victim of one of the other
hunters. A beautiful dark grizzly and an elk also joined the
bag, as well as three more goats.

In six days the potential for game was exhausted
there, so we moved camp with our twenty-eight horses to the
Top of the World. The Top of the World is a plateau, almost
flat, with an elevation near timberline at seven thousand
feet. The open meadows were literally torn up with grizzly
digging. There were no elk or moose on the plateau itself,
but plenty of mule deer. This was to be our grizzly camp. It
hadn't been hunted for more than forty years.

The first day there Don senior and Jim came back in
the evening with the hide of a good bear, and they had seen
three others. Don junior had missed a bull elk down in the
Coyote Creek bottom north of camp. He had a moose dead
to rights in an open meadow by the creek, but couldn't find
the bull in his telescope sight!

The following day Don senior killed a big mule deer
continued on page 117

FATHER DE SMET, IN HIS LETTERS TO HIS BISHOP IN 1846,
WROTE OF THE EAST KOOTENAY, "ON COMING OUT OF THE TIMBER,
THE MOUNTAINS RISE UP LIKE THUNDER."

❖ ❖ ❖

FEE HELLMEN'S FIRST BIG GAME, A BEAR, FALL 1934.

WARDNER, B.C., AROUND THE TIME OF FEE HELLMEN'S BIRTH THERE IN 1918.

FEE HELLMEN HEWING LOGS, 1938.

ALTA AT THE AGE OF SEVENTEEN.

ALTA AND A SMALL BUCK IN 1939.

IN THE DAYS OF THE DEPRESSION,
DEER WERE OFTEN KILLED TWO AT A TIME FOR FOOD.

ANTLERS FROM FEE'S FIRST ELK, 1939.

YOUNG BRYAN AND GARY HELLMEN DISCUSSING THE KILL.

THE HELLMEN CHILDREN GARY, RAY, LYNN AND BRYAN, 1948.

GARY (WEARING PACK) AND BRYAN HELLMEN
LEARN THE RUDIMENTS OF BACKPACKING IN 1955.

FEE HELLMEN VIEWS A RAINBOW ON A DAY'S OUTING UP PERRY CREEK.

FRANK MANNERS (LEFT) AND FEE HELLMEN HOLDING SHEEP HEAD, AFTER A LONG, HARD HUNT.

buck up on the slope of Sugar Loaf Peak. Prepared for just such an eventuality, Jim carried a coil of heavy telephone wire and a pair of pliers in his pack. The kill was in an ideal spot for bear bait, just below the crest of a saddle, except that there was nothing substantial to wire it to. The small spruces there were shallow-rooted. But moving the kill down into heavier growth was not advisable, either, for there would be no way of coming up on it without alerting the bear, if bear there should be. After caping the animal, Jim wired the carcass securely to one of the small spruces.

Two days after the deer kill we decided that Don junior and I should check it. Jim had some camp chores to attend to, so Don senior was to guide us to the kill.

We left camp just after daybreak. The grasses in the meadow in front of camp were white with hoarfrost, but the sky was clear and it promised to be a glorious day. Game trails carved out by the hoofs of the deer were plentiful and well defined. Timber at this altitude was sparse and scrubby, so the going was good. The deciduous foliage was blazing with color. The tang of the upland spruce was in our nostrils. As the Indians used to say, it was a good day to die!

We proceeded slowly because of Don junior's bad knee. We shivered a bit in the keen air, but once the sun rose over the eastern crags we took off our coats and proceeded in shirtsleeves. It was my habit to carry my own rifle for backup any time I had only one hunter in grizzly country, but it was awkward carrying two rifles slung on the shoulders as well as a day-pack full of binoculars, water bottle, photographic gear, lunches, and so on. Depending upon Jim's glowing accounts of Don senior's shooting ability, I dispensed for the day with my own rifle.

It was nearly two hours before we topped a small peak, rather a knob, and could get our first look at the area where the deer was supposed to be. The slope before us was concave, the summit of the ridge sweeping back and dropping slightly before it soared upward to form Sugar Loaf Peak. One look over the knob told us that the deer was gone. There were no birds about, and there should have been a flock of Clark's nutcrackers in attendance. But down in the tops of some higher growth they were screaming and fluttering. Don senior pointed out the spot where the deer had been left, but a good scan with the binoculars showed definitely that it had been moved.

Dropping back behind the ridge, we maneuvered into the slight saddle between the knob and Sugar Loaf. A big game trail came through there, and in the trail were the marks of huge pads. A sober thought convinced me that we should back off. A small, shaly draw lay between us and the birds, and there was no way we could cross that shale without alerting the bear — if he were still on the bait. The thermal breezes were fitful with the change in temperature from night to day, so a vagrant downdraft would give us away. My reasoning was that the bear would be long gone unless he chose to protect his cache. If he opted to remain and argue the point, we were rather at a disadvantage, considering Don junior's bad knee and his inexperience. True, Don senior had Jim's endorsement, but I couldn't be sure what his reaction would be in a tight situation. I would have felt better if I had had my own rifle.

Just then came the rending crash of breaking wood from the timber. The sound echoed back to us from Sugar Loaf. The birds rose in a cloud. The bear was down there. Judging from the racket he made, and the size of his tracks, he was no weakling.

Don senior turned, grinning, toward me. "Let's go get him!" he whispered.

"I think we should study this for a minute," I whispered back, and I outlined my apprehension, omitting my thoughts on possible personal shortcomings. "I've come two thousand miles to shoot a bear," Don junior objected. "I'm not backing off when I can hear one this close." And he took his rifle from my shoulder and led off, hobbling down the mountain.

We moved down slowly, Don junior in the lead, followed closely by Don senior, and me in the rear. We crossed the shale, making unavoidable noise. The birds flew off at our approach, giving another tip to the bear. The drag trail was clear. We came into a little gloomy glade amongst the trees, and there, seventy feet away on the other side, was the bear's cache — a typical mound of dirt, the area for many feet in every direction torn up to supply material. No sign of the bear. I had a feeling of relief but it lasted only a moment.

A huge head shoved up from behind the mound, and the next second the bear came over the top.

This was my first encounter with a charging grizzly, and he didn't act at all as I had imagined one would. He didn't roar. He just gave out deep-chested grunts, not unlike a pig. He didn't come flat-out, moving fast as a bear can. He came deliberately, sidling, head swinging from side to side with each step, low, but with nose pointed upward at us, teeth popping between grunts. I had the feeling that if we had turned tail and run away, he would not have pursued us. But if we stood to meet him, he was more than willing.

Both hunters shouldered their rifles. I thought Don junior would never shoot. The bear was nearly on him before he pulled the trigger.

Click! It didn't fire!

Then Don senior's rifle roared. The bear collapsed in a heap, scrambled immediately to his feet, and headed straight downhill at full speed. Just at the edge of the clearing he crashed straight into the bole of a large tree, recoiled, and disappeared into the brush.

We were all shaking from the close call. "What went wrong with your rifle, Don?" I asked.

"Misfire, I guess."

"No, I know what happened," Don senior confessed. "I was wandering around camp last night and decided to check all the rifles. I found yours with the magazine loaded and a round in the chamber. I thought that wasn't safe around camp, so I took the cartridge out of the chamber."

"And you forgot to tell me about it!"

"Yes, I guess that's right."

I was feeling pretty sheepish too. To let my hunters go into a situation like that without asking them to check their rifles first was unforgivable.

We had come out of this encounter well enough, but now we had a sorely wounded bear to contend with. In our next skirmish he might not be so slow, nor in an open space. It was also possible we might lose him altogether.

I was puzzled by the bear's actions following the shot. He had fallen as though he had been hit in the head, but he was leaving a bright blood trail, which suggested a punctured lung. Still, it had been a frontal shot and his head had been low in front of his chest, so that didn't make sense. He wouldn't have dropped from a lung shot, either. He was running blind, crashing head-on into the boles of the larger trees, and once he had landed fair in the crotch of a big jack pine that forked near the ground. In spite of the steepness of the terrain he was still accelerating, and his claws were turning up clods of duff at each leap.

After a couple of hundred yards or so he slowed and

stopped hitting the larger obstructions. He began following the many game trails for short distances, thereby zigzagging down the mountain. Obviously he was regaining his senses.

We came on him, however, lying in the midst of a thicket of low willows, on his belly, his hind feet sticking out behind. Don junior brushed past me when I stopped to take a reading on the situation.

"Hold on, Don, he's still breathing!" I could see his flanks heaving as he attempted to pump air. But surely he was unconscious. "Better shoot him again!" When I got a good look at him I added, "Don't shoot him in the head! He looks big enough to make the Record Book!"

Don junior shot him once behind the shoulder. Don senior's 180-grain Silvertip bullet had struck the grizzly fair in the left nostril. It tore out all his top teeth on that side and glanced down the air passages into the lungs. Reason enough for him to hit the ground and bleed so copiously.

Back at camp that night I pulled another boner, a real dilly. The skull of that massive beast was by far the largest any of us had ever seen. I skinned it out but left the cleaning and fleshing of it for the next day. I laid it on the top of a stump behind the cabin, and the next morning it was gone. Our best guess was that a wandering wolverine had carted it off during the night.

A few years later, in 1960, another of my hunters, Frank Nataros of Claresholm, Alberta, did break into the Boone and Crockett *Records of North American Big Game* (posted in 1964) with a big grizzly taken on Noke Creek, but it was not nearly so large as Don junior's Top-of-the-World grizzly.

The Man from Missouri

❖　　❖　　❖

FRANK MANNERS AND I LAY on our bellies at the edge of timberline, on a hogback ridge separating Two-Buck Basin from the Wild Horse River. We were glassing for bighorn rams.

This was the area where a huge ram was killed by Scotty MacDougall in the winter of 1892–93. Its horns supposedly measured 52½ inches around the curl, and 18½ inches around the base. Pictures of the head still exist, but the head itself was burned when a fire destroyed W. F. Sheard's taxidermy studio in Tacoma, Washington. There is much debate as to its authenticity.

Be that as it may, there were still some magnificent rams around, and we lay in the midst of their home territory. The clean, sharp air gave us the best in visibility. Somber gray peaks surrounded us on every hand, with vast grassy slopes clothing the open basins. Far below us ran the silvery ribbon of the Wild Horse in its narrow, rocky gorge. Between it and the ridge we were on, the mountain shoulders were clothed in the somber greens of the spruce forest. The deciduous trees and shrubs were blazing with color: the sky was a vivid blue. Who wouldn't envy the sheep their fall pasture?

Just by chance I spotted an animal as he passed over a skyline away to the south. It was so far away that even through my powerful Bushnells I couldn't have told what species of animal it was, except that the head looked heavy and blunt. A bighorn ram!

The sighting of that ram triggered the action for what turned out to be the most grueling as well as the most interesting day I ever spent in the mountains.

Frank was from Missouri, an instructor in the Marines, and a tough, resourceful man. I was working as a guide for Harry Bjorn, outfitter, and had been paired off with Frank. It was our second fall hunt together, although it was Frank's fourteenth try for a full-curl ram. So far he had been denied a full curl, although he had taken a smaller one on his first hunt.

There had been problems in those other years in finding a guide who could keep up with Frank in the rugged Hughes Range, and I was trying my best to fill the bill. I had the reputation as a tough man myself — not macho tough, but able to hike and climb and backpack beyond the average. It was interesting that while Frank could walk away from me on a trail, I surpassed him slightly when it came to rock climbing. All in all, we were well matched. It was inevitable that a friendly rivalry should spring up between us as to who was the better man. Thus far we hadn't had the opportunity to settle the matter.

Our undeclared rivalry had taken on an international flavor, too. We were both proud of our respective homelands, and missed no opportunity to needle each other in a friendly way. One day I had broken open a fresh pack of Canadian cigarettes. "How much do you pay for a pack of those?" Frank asked.

"Dollar twenty."

"Wow!" Pretending amazement, Frank brought forth a pack of Camels. "Do you know what I paid for these down home?"

"No."

"Eighty cents. Boy, are you guys dumb!"

A short time later he offered me one of his Camels.

"No, thanks," I refused. "I never smoke those cheap cigarettes." From time to time thereafter he would offer me one of his Camels, and of course I always refused.

I told Frank about the ram I had seen, and where. There were four basins between us and the skyline where I had spotted him, and he had disappeared in the fifth. I couldn't believe it at first when Frank said, "Let's go get him!"

"You've got to be kidding," I protested. "It will take us until dark just to get over there!"

"Then we'll have to stay out overnight and shoot him in the morning!"

One ram traveling alone wasn't liable to stop before he had found others of his kind, and probably when we looked over into the basin where he had disappeared he would be long gone. Also, one ram traveling alone was not likely to be of very great size. Frank knew all these things as well as I, and clearly he had thrown out a challenge. I couldn't back down.

One thing in our favor was the good weather. The morning was crisp and cool, early October, and with our traditional Indian summer in full swing, the weather wasn't likely to change. A night on the mountain wouldn't do us any harm, although I was an ardent lover of my eiderdown sleeping bag.

Our only preparation for the ordeal ahead was to

remove our jackets and stuff them into the bag on my packboard.

We trotted down the long, steep game trail into the bottom of Two-Buck Basin, losing nearly a thousand feet in elevation. We crossed over a heavily wooded ridge into the First Triple Basin. Up past the Horse Creek waterfall into the Second Triple Basin. Across the nearly level bottom of it, weaving our way through the moss-covered, house-size boulders, and up the long, heart-bursting climb over treacherous, rotten rock ledges to a summit overlooking Davis Basin.

We paused there briefly to eat our lunch and then, still chewing the last bite, ran in great bounds down a loose shale slide into the bottom of Davis. We pushed our way through a thicket of clutching alders past Davis Lake, and struggled up a long, boulder-strewn slope to the crest of the final saddle.

We were both wringing wet with sweat; on the worst of the climbs I thought either my heart or my lungs would burst. I felt much as I thought a marathon runner must feel when nearing the finish line. But there were signs of strain on Frank's face too. Soon, at this pace, one or the other of us would have to falter.

From the lip of the saddle we were now on, a wide ledge led off to the right with a sheer bluff standing above it — a perfect camouflage background for us. The ledge was low, perhaps forty feet above a long, grassy slope running down to the bottom of the basin where our early-morning ram had disappeared. Off to our left the basin broke up into a series of dark ledges and beetling cliffs.

We could hardly believe the scene below us. Way down in a little yellow meadow with a small stream coursing through it were seventeen rams! We could see more

moving about, feeding in a sparse thicket of alpine larch —
about twenty-two in all, we thought. Such a large group
was unusual. Mostly they traveled in flocks of five to seven
or eight. Probably several bands had met here by accident,
and this theory was born out a little later. Through the
binoculars I made out at least five full-curls amongst them.

Lying off a bit by himself was the biggest of the
sheep. He lay on a little gray moraine knoll like the King of
the Castle, and I suppose he was. He had an extremely
heavy, wide, sweeping curl, and his lamb points seemed
intact. He had without a doubt the biggest head either of us
had ever seen.

The range was really much too far for a sure shot,
but my watch showed it to be four o'clock. Either we had to
chance the long shot or stay out overnight in the hope they
would still be there in the morning, a most unlikely prospect.
Given time, we could have made a good stalk around
through the bluffs to our left and come on them at a much
lower elevation, and consequently closer range.

Contrary to our expectations of the weather for the
day, a wicked front had moved in and clouds were hovering
low overhead. Moreover, thunder was muttering in those
clouds, with a heavier crack from time to time as a bolt
struck somewhere amongst the peaks, throwing wild echoes
back and forth. With only our eyeballs showing over the
edge of the ledge, we put on our jackets against the cold
breeze. Wet with sweat, we were already beginning to shiver.

Frank flopped down and crawled ahead until only
his head and rifle peeped over the brink. I set up my
binoculars and tripod behind him so I was looking right
down over his gun barrel.

He turned his head to me. "How far?" he mouthed.
It was hard to make a good guess over the sweeping terrain.

I shrugged. "Five hundred yards?"

"How much do you think I should hold over?"

He was shooting a .300 H&H Magnum. The trajectory should be much the same as my .270 Winchester, although I had no idea what range his rifle was sighted for.

"Two feet."

He studied for a minute. "Think I'll make it three."

He settled behind his scope. Just before I put my eye to the binoculars I noticed a fist-sized rock directly in front of his muzzle. His scope, being a trifle higher than the bore, cleared the top of the rock.

"Hold it!" I cautioned, and pointed to the rock. If he had fired, we would have been rewarded by a cloud of rock dust in front of our faces.

Frank moved a foot or two to one side, then settled down again to shoot. When he fired I saw the slug hit the shale just inches over the ram's back. In an instant the whole flock had jumped to their feet. They ran up into a close group as tight as they could stand, each with its head held over the back of its immediate neighbor. That had to be the most thrilling sight I ever witnessed! Twenty or so big rams pressed tightly together, massive horns raised high!

Of course we expected them all to take off down the basin, but instead they stood for a few moments, then gradually spread out again. Clearly, with the thunder crashing amongst the peaks, the sound of the shot and the echoes it set up, they were confused.

They all spread out again, and Frank took another shot at the big one. This time I didn't see where the bullet struck, but as before they all rushed into a tight knot, chins on each other's backs. They spread out again, and Frank had another opportunity. Another miss.

Now they all broke down the basin, running hard

through the rocks as only a sheep can run, their white fannies bobbing and weaving. The big one was in the lead, unscathed.

Then, to corroborate our belief that there was more than one group involved, five rams cut out of the flock, made a reverse turn up onto the grassy slope, and came right back to us. The leader of these looked to be a good one — not nearly as big as the one Frank had hoped for, but still carrying a full curl. They came right up to within a hundred yards of us, and directly below. There, still unaware of our presence, they stopped to study the situation. Frank, with the last cartridge in his magazine, shot the leader.

He fell just at the base of the cliffs on our left. We climbed down to perform a hurried caping operation and of course take a measurement of the horns. The results were disappointing. The curl was close, and measured out at thirty-six inches for the right horn, thirty-seven for the left. The horns were heavily broomed. The bases were fifteen and a half inches.

Frank cut the hams off at the hip joint. With a piece of rope I had in my pack, he tied the hocks together and slung them over his shoulder. I saw this to be an act calculated to ensure that his burden was approximately equal to mine, with the big head. Fair was fair, and we hadn't yet come to any conclusion as to who was the better man.

With our loads it was a hard climb back up to the ledge from which Frank had shot, and just before we reached it we sat down for a short breather. Frank let the rope off his shoulder, and automatically we began peering through our binoculars at the surrounding country. As we were thus engaged, the two hams started rolling unnoticed. By the time we realized what had happened, they were well on their way down to the little meadow.

I think any man other than Frank would have left
them there for the scavengers, but he climbed down probably two hundred yards, slung them back on his shoulder, and
returned slowly up that terrible slope. And it was not as if we
needed the meat. Others of our party had been successful,
and there was plenty in camp.

Now consider: in the morning we had made a stiff
climb of a thousand vertical feet or better up to the hogback
from where I had first seen the ram. Then we had negotiated
four big basins with the expenditure of tremendous effort,
shot the ram in the fifth. We still had to make our way back
to camp burdened with fifty to sixty pounds each on our
backs, unless we decided to bivouac. We had no proper
clothing for a night on the mountain. It was now very cold
and windy at our elevation, and the sky suggested rain or
snow before morning. Obviously we should try to make
it back, and besides, we were still wondering who was the
better man.

Of course it was impossible to return the way we
had come. It had taken us from daylight in the morning
until four in the afternoon going all out to get to the basin
where Frank shot the ram. Now it was after five, and
darkness not far off. But by cutting straight down to the Wild
Horse from the bottom of Davis Basin we would find the
pack trail that followed up the stream, and walk it about
four miles to camp, thus bypassing three of the four basins.

We were making our way along a small dry wash
halfway down Davis Basin at dusk, when three beautiful
rams came out below us. They had heard us, but were unsure
what or where we were. They came out of a thicket of shin-
tangle and crossed the wash about a hundred yards below
us. As they crossed we could see that one of them had a bad
limp in the right hind leg. He also carried a first-rate head,

a full, wide curl. Not so large as the one Frank had missed, but still an outstanding trophy. They stood on a small game trail at the edge of the wash, broadside on.

Harry Bjorn had told me to be on the lookout for this particular ram. One of Harry's hunters had wounded him in the hip a couple of years before, but he had escaped and recovered. He had been seen several times since, always in impossible situations. Now we had him at our mercy except for one thing: I already had a ram's head on my packboard.

We watched that magnificent dark ram for a good minute before he moved into the brush. We had three more hunters in camp, all with sheep tags, and it spoke volumes for Frank's sense of sportsmanship that he didn't lower the boom on that great beast.

It was completely dark before we reached the bottom of Davis Basin. We struggled through the brush and blow-down, always leery of falling over a small hidden ledge, working toward the sound of the brawling Wild Horse below. We waded the river and climbed the opposite bank in such utter darkness that we knew we had found the pack trail only by the level feel beneath our feet. Only four more miles to go! But all uphill.

I was nearing the limit of my endurance. The trail was rough, full of exposed roots and rocks. We stumbled on in what can be described only as agony. The trail hadn't been cut out that year, and from time to time we came to windfalls across it — big, limby spruce for the most part. We had worked the horses around these obstacles on the way in, sometimes up the slope, sometimes down, but in the darkness it was not possible to see which way was better. We had to clamber around them as well as we could, and I had one painful fall in the process. It's one thing to fall without a burden, something else with fifty to sixty pounds strapped to the shoulders!

Never was there such a cheerful sight as the fire when we finally reached the edge of the meadow at camp. Another half-mile and I'm sure I couldn't have made it. We staggered into the firelight at a quarter to midnight. I was so exhausted that my voice came out in hoarse croaks. I dropped my packboard with the beautiful head beside the fire, where the rest of the party was still waiting up for us, and staggered to a seat. Frank slid the hams from his shoulder. His shoulders must have been raw from the chafing rope, but he never let on.

He walked over to the table where a bottle of bourbon whiskey stood, and poured two stiff drinks. I had never seen him take a drink in the two years I had been his guide. He brought one over to me.

"My birthday today," he said.

Then with a big smile on his face, he pulled out his pack of Camels and offered me one.

"Thanks," I croaked, "Believe I will. Congratulations!"

IV

❖ ❖ ❖

GUIDING ON THE MOYIE

Guide, Class A

❖   ❖   ❖

ON AN EVENING IN SEPTEMBER, 1961, I walked down to Guido Benedetti's corner store for a package of cigarettes. Guido was talking with a couple of men who were togged out in the usual hunter's paraphernalia: red woolen shirts, high boots, knives on their belts, and the inevitable red fluorescent caps.

Guido looked up as I entered the store. "Here's the man you're looking for," he said to the men. "Fee, meet the Nataros brothers. This is Harry, better known as 'Doc,' from Langley, and this is Frank, from Claresholm.

"They want to hunt here together, since Cranbrook is halfway between their homes. Frank is a nonresident, so they need a guide. Could you help them out?"

I could see several objections to the proposal. In the first place, though I had guided on a few trips under Jim White and Harry Bjorn, I had no hunting territory of my own. A Class B guide, as I was, had to work under a Class A outfitter, who had to have a registered area in which to operate.

I had no outfit except the normal hunter's kit, no tents, cooking utensils, nor a hundred and one other necessities. The greatest need was for a string of horses to transport hunters and equipment into the hinterland, wherever an outfitter's territory happened to be. In the East Kootenay all the outfitters had strings of ten to twenty horses. Hunting without horses had never been tried with nonresident hunters, to the best of my knowledge. I could probably have rented horses and equipment, but I am not and never was a horseman. I hunted with White and Bjorn on the understanding that I would not be required to handle horses, but would try to pull my weight at camp chores, for which I was better fitted.

I was a very good hunter, I got along well with the clients, and perhaps I had more than my share of good luck. The hunters in my charge always seemed to do exceedingly well.

Then, too, when I met the Nataros brothers, I was working as a clerk in the old Farmer's Co-op, and even though I was overdue for an annual vacation, it would be unfair to my employers to leave on such short notice.

"What game are you interested in?" I asked Doc.

"Well, just about anything legal," he answered. "We would like a goat or two, and a grizzly if the opportunity came along."

I pointed out the problems I could foresee. Possibly I could prevail on either Bjorn or White to book them and hire me as a guide. But since they were already out in the mountains with parties, it would be hard to contact them and set up the deal. And of course their horses would already be in use.

"Don't worry about horses," Doc said. "We're not horsemen. In fact, we'd rather hunt on foot if there is any place we could go without horses. We have a camper, and we'd just like to go somewhere we can drive to and live in the camper. The main thing is for the two of us to be outdoors together for a spell."

That settled two of the problems right there. Most local hunters, including me, did quite well without horses. There was no real reason why strangers to the area couldn't do as well, if they had a guide who knew the country. However, there still remained the problem of a territory to make things legal.

For the rest of the evening I mulled things over. They wanted goats, and I knew of a small band that ranged in the Moyie Canyon, just above where the highway crosses the river ten miles from Cranbrook. I had discovered this little band three years before. It was a most unlikely spot in which to find goats, miles from any other true goat habitat, and because of their isolation from others of their kind, they would be very vulnerable to local hunting pressure if resident hunters knew about them, so I had kept the knowledge to myself. I had killed one goat there the year I discovered them, and Bryan had taken his first goat, a big old billy, there a couple of years later. I thought the band could stand to lose another one or two.

The next day I went to see Ross Farquharson, then the senior wildlife official in town, and enquired about getting a territory.

"There are just none available," he said. "Every area is taken up through the whole East Kootenay."

"How about the Moyie?" I outlined the Nataros brothers' interests and mentioned the little band of goats. Ross knew of my work with the other guides, and that I was qualified for a Class A license provided a territory was available.

"Man, that's rough country for horses. Windfalls and brush thicker than hair on a dog. That's why no one else has considered it. And as soon as you cut trails for the horses the local hunters would be up there in droves. But I could give it to you if you want it."

"I don't intend to use horses," I explained. "It wouldn't pay me to keep a string of horses the year around just for a few weeks' hunting. I intend to hunt it just the same as local hunters do. Camp close to the old roads, and hunt within backpacking distance. Two hours from Cranbrook and the hunters would be in action."

Ross reflected for a minute. "You might have something there," he said. "I could give you the Moyie above Lumberton, Lamb Creek above Mineral Lake, and Perry Creek above Old Town. Plenty of game on those three. Lots of bear, both black and grizzly. Good for moose, too, and some caribou. Elk are spreading up both the Moyie and Lamb Creek. Hey, that sounds pretty good. And the goats you mentioned. They won't stand much hunting pressure, so go easy on them. But there are more goats up near Cooper Lake and the headwaters of Perry Creek. It's a hell of a hard country to get around in, though."

The main road up the Moyie was not built beyond Weaver Creek at that time, but there were old roads dating back to the late twenties and early thirties running away up some of the tributaries where the Lumberton White Spruce sawmill complex had operated. Most of those roads were all but impassable, but I thought a little work on them would make them usable for my old Ford pickup.

The rough, overgrown roads were to my advantage, really. In those days there was a lot of game just about anywhere in the East Kootenay, so the local hunters could go wherever the traveling was good with almost a certainty of getting game. They wouldn't be likely to tackle those rough roads, so they shouldn't be a bother.

The Moyie had been burned off in the thirties in what must have been a terrific conflagration. The ground was strewn with huge windfalls, and had grown up thickly with willow, alder, and jack pine. It made for tough hunting. It was not pretty country, no alpine basins or big, open slides such as in the Rockies to the east, but I was sure there was lots of game.

Following my meeting with Farquharson I went to see my boss, Howard King. It was a slack time business-wise, and he gave me a week off. Then I met again with the Nataros brothers, and we struck a deal. They were to pay me twenty dollars a day (more than my wages at the Co-op at the time), assume all expenses, and do the cooking. Even though I didn't come out too well financially, at least it meant a change of pace for me, doing what I loved best. It was a decent enough deal all the way around.

The next day they had two goats within two hours of leaving Cranbrook. The following day we moved up toward Cooper Lake as far as we could drive, and there they killed a big mule deer buck. We saw three grizzlies that eluded us, and they passed up a bull moose.

In the meantime I had the opportunity to size up at least a small portion of my new hunting territory, and I was amazed at the variety and amount of game there was. The next three years were going to be very interesting.

The brothers booked again for the following year, and went home happy.

My Territory

❖   ❖   ❖

AFTER THE SNOW HAD GONE from the Moyie Valley the next spring, 1962, I began spending every weekend scouting my new hunting territory.

I couldn't consider making a living as a guide; the season was too short. Guiding would have to remain a hobby, with some remuneration — a sort of vacation with pay.

As a matter of fact, I hadn't had a real holiday in more than ten years. I just couldn't afford it. There was no vacation pay in those days. I'd been taking time off in the fall to work as a guide for other outfitters, and it was a welcome change but hard work and full of responsibility. Having my own territory really wouldn't change my life that much.

To get acquainted with the Moyie was enough for the summer. Again I was amazed at the amount of game there was. The headwaters of Noke, Lewisby, and Ridgeway creeks — all smaller tributaries of the Moyie — and of course the far reaches of the Moyie proper, showed particular promise. I concentrated on finding pockets close to the old roads, where the going wasn't too bad. One day in

August, while the rest of the family picked huckleberries, I made a wide sweep through the mountains around Cooper Lake. It would be impossible to pack meat out of there on my back, but I wanted to study the potential for bear. Nobody wanted bear meat, so the hides would be the only burden.

I climbed to the mountain summit on the north, following the height of land around a big double cirque until I was west of the lake. I walked through acre after acre of huckleberries, and it looked as though every bear in North America had been feeding on them. Piles of purple dung were everywhere. At the elevation I was traveling there was much open country with no windfalls. Grizzly diggings, where they had been after gophers, were common on these open slopes. There were claw marks high on some of the trees, showing that some of the bears were mighty big.

Since I was not interested in killing anything that day, I had left my rifle at home. Neither was I interested in actually seeing game. Studying the sign as I went would give me the information I needed. Only once had I seen more bear sign, and that was at the Top of the World between Lussier and Coyote Creek in the Rockies when I had guided one fall for Jim White. That bear sign was concentrated in the Top of the World meadows, a relatively small area compared to the ground I covered this August day.

Late in the afternoon I found myself on the height of land west of Cooper Lake. It had been my intention to cut down to the lake, where I would find a trail leading back to the huckleberry pickers. My direct route to the lake was through a tremendous jungle of alders. Anyone who has traveled in the mountains knows all about alders. They grow in a heavily intertwined fashion, the lower portion growing out horizontally before the tops sweep upward to a height of up to twenty feet. The horizontal bases create a horrible impediment, akin to climbing through a dense mat of windfalls. Vision is often restricted to only a few yards.

During the early part of the day I had kept pretty well to the open where I could see in every direction. I had also made plenty of noise. No way did I wish to come suddenly upon a grizzly, possibly a female with cubs, or stumble on one feeding on some carrion. Without the familiar comfort of my rifle, I was taking no chances.

The only alternative to traversing this jungle was a long detour to the south. That would mean negotiating some mighty rough rock ledges, and it would be dark before I could get through them. I would have to go through the alder thicket. Not until later was I to find a winding channel through that thicket, with good going all the way to the meadows at the lake.

To my surprise, when I got to the alders I found game trails lacing all through them. Bear trails. Dung everywhere. Bear odor heavy on the air. Night was coming on quickly. I can't say I was frightened, but I was mighty uneasy. Fortunately the trails made for rapid passage, and with much whistling I hurried along until I reached the lake and the trail. It was completely dark when I rejoined my family at our camp.

At that time the elk didn't range much above Lewisby Creek, but on Weaver Creek there was much sign. A big, marshy draw on the north side of Ridgeway Creek was simply cut up with moose tracks. Later we named this draw the Moose Pasture. There were goats all along the rimrock between Moyie and Irishman creeks, and a quick trip up to the headwaters of Perry Creek showed that moose ranged there, too. There were no sheep on this side of the

Kootenay, but caribou wandered all through the boreal forests in all the watersheds.

In June I began getting enquiries from hunters. The usual procedure for potential hunters was to write to the Fish and Wildlife Department in Victoria, British Columbia, asking for the names of guides in the area they wished to hunt. Of course my name was amongst them. I answered these letters in all honesty, pointing out that I didn't use horses, that the country was hard to hunt, and that any hunters I took on must be in top physical condition. I would have to be allowed a free day following a kill so I could hump the meat out on my back. As it turned out there were only two occasions in the next three years when that was necessary — not because they didn't get any game, but in most cases the kill was made near a road and extensive packing wasn't necessary.

Oddly enough, most hunters enjoyed the savage pastime of backpacking. I kept spare packboards on hand, and the hunters thought it was a great adventure to hump out a part of their own game. I was pleasantly surprised, too, at how many of my clients shared my attitude toward horses, and on that account wished to avail themselves of the services I offered.

Since I didn't have a herd of horses to feed over winter and didn't need the services of a horse-wrangler, I could operate much more cheaply. The going rate at that time for a pack trip was in the neighborhood of sixty dollars per man-day. I quoted forty.

I planned short-order meals (but not out of cans), and I did the cooking when I had only two hunters. If I had more I hired my wife, Alta, as cook and an old woodsman friend, John Avis, as assistant guide.

I had Mary, the wife of Frank Whitehead, chief of

the St. Mary's Indian band, make me two tepees of Egyptian cotton. One was twelve feet in diameter and weighed five pounds. The other was sixteen feet in diameter and weighed ten pounds. I also bought a good cottage-style tent. I set up permanent tepee poles at all my camps, so it only took ten minutes to set up a tepee and have a fire started in it.

All grub and equipment other than the hunters' personal gear were packed in the day before my clients' arrival. Within two hours of leaving Cranbrook they were settled comfortably in the tepees. They thought it was marvelous and so romantic! And within two hours of the hunt's termination they were back in town. I allowed a minimum of four days between trips, two to recuperate physically and two to set up camp for the next hopefuls.

I booked only one party that fall in addition to the Nataros brothers. They, too were brothers, from California. It turned out to be a terribly wet fall, and it rained for the whole ten days of their trip. They did get a caribou, an elk, and a fine mule deer. Not a big bag, but satisfactory considering the conditions. They were pleased enough to book again for the following year.

Then one day after they had gone, I had a call from Ed Wood at Park's Hardware. He said an old Texan had come into the store enquiring whether it was possible to hire a guide for a few days. An off-the-cuff hunt like that was impossible to book with the regular guides, as time was too short to allow rounding up horses and generally organizing the hunt. I was ready to go in a matter of hours.

I went down to Park's to meet the Texan. He was a tall, thin old man, complete with Stetson hat and cowboy boots, who must have been crowding eighty. I told him the country was too rough for a man of his age. He insisted that the main thing was to get out in the mountains for a spell.

Shooting game wasn't too important, money was no object, and so on.

I wangled another week off from work, and away we went. There were lots of grouse that year, and we often saw them along the roads. The Texan had an old Winchester pump action shotgun, twelve gauge, worn shiny with use, and could that old boy shoot! I would stop the truck when we came to a covey. He would get out and load his gun, then walk up on the birds until they flew. The roads were narrow, but the Winchester came up smoothly, there would be a cloud of feathers at the shot, and we had another grouse for the pot. Twice I saw him make doubles. Fantastic shooting!

On the third day when we were eating breakfast he said, "Well, Fee, I just can't get around in these windfalls. How about you going out today and shooting me a grizzly and a caribou?"

"No way," I answered. "It's illegal, and besides, I just can't see how anybody could enjoy a trophy his guide killed."

"Well, I thought I would like to take something home with me so I could b.s. my friends. I thought all guides killed game for their hunters."

"Not in this country, they don't. Sorry."

"I guess we'd better pack up, then."

"You realize that you booked for five days? You'll have to pay for the full trip, so we may as well put in the whole time."

"Oh, no problem." And he pulled out a thick wallet and counted out ten twenties. He started to put his wallet back in his pocket, then pulled it out again. "Here," he said, and handed me another twenty. "I enjoyed the trip, and I know you did the best that you could for me."

I thought it must be nice to own an oil well or two.

I have to say a word or two here for my wife and our family. When Alta cooked for me on these trips, she really took a beating. She was holding down a responsible, nerve-racking job on the order desk for Scott National Fruit Company. She would get up in the morning at camp, get breakfast for us, wash the dishes, make lunches, then drive to town in her old black Chev over those rough roads and put in an exhausting day on the order desk. Then back over the cobbles to have our supper (dinner if you prefer) ready by the time we got back to camp. Dirty dishes again in the evening, and a repeat performance the next day.

Our daughter, Lynn, then going to Mount Baker High School, kept the home fires burning, cooking, cleaning, and generally looking after our three boys, who were also in high school at the time. The boys in turn took care of the man's chores around the home and in the evenings they set ten-pins at the old Venezia Bowling Alley. None of us had much time for frivolity.

It's funny but we never did get rich.

The Tepee

❖   ❖   ❖

DOC NATAROS AND I HAD HUNTED the big, rocky height between the headwaters of the North Fork of the Moyie and Perry Creek on a blustery wet day in late October. We had put in a miserable ten hours, but soon we would reach camp. We had not seen one head of game in the entire day, and we were cold, tired, wet, hungry, and discouraged.

We came out on the rimrock overlooking camp. Even as we stood there the clouds parted, and a shaft of welcome sunlight slowly illuminated the meadow below us. Our tepee stood out, a bright white cone with its smoke-darkened tip in the middle of the bright green meadow. Beyond the meadow the mountain fell away far toward the darkly timbered valley of the North Fork. It was one of those beautiful scenes that one sometimes comes upon, and it held us spellbound for several minutes.

The focus of our attention was the tepee. In it was warmth, food, shelter from the vicious wind and rain, and all we needed to restore our spirits. A few minutes after we had scrambled down from the rimrock we had a fire in the tepee, our wet clothing was hung to dry on the supporting poles, the warmth of the small fire was reflecting off the walls and seeping into our frigid bones, and we sat on our sleeping bags contentedly sipping hot toddies.

The tepee, of course, is an invention of the Native nomads of North America. Through the centuries they refined it in a hundred different ways until it became eminently suited to their needs. Admittedly it is not so efficient as, say, a wall-tent with a stove inside, and it has many drawbacks that the modern camper would find nearly intolerable. But the Indians, by carefully selecting their campsites, avoided many of these.

Proper fuel was one of their prime concerns. They therefore had to choose a site where they could select wood that gave off little smoke, burned cleanly, and didn't throw off sparks that would burn holes in their equipment. Probably the worst, because of its sparking tendency, is the wood and bark of the tamarack. The best is the heavy bark of the fir. Wood of the deciduous trees is nearly as good. Birch, aspen, willow, and alder are all fine. Somewhere in the middle are the woods of jack pine, balsam, and spruce.

Smoke in the tepee is an unavoidable nuisance, although not nearly so bad as is generally supposed. Anyone who has sat around an outdoor fire with an eddying breeze blowing knows all about smarting eyes, choking smoke, and the danger from popping sparks. In a tepee the air is still.

I once endured a hunting trip where we slept in a factory-built tepee. Luckily we had a few extra lengths of stove pipe to spare. By cutting a stove out of a square five-gallon coal-oil can, and running the stove pipe up through the smoke hole, we survived. No self-respecting Indian would have been caught dead in that factory-built concoction. It simply wouldn't draw.

My two tepees seemed to be identical except for size. But the smaller one drew much better than the larger one, for what reason I never could fathom. Mary Whitehead, who made them for me, told me that this was common. Perhaps a modern parallel would be two cars identical in make and model, where one out-performs the other.

No Indian would have selected the site where Nataros and I had our camp. I wouldn't have either, if I'd had a choice. This spot was close to the only water for miles, and we therefore had to be content with it. The wind eddied down in the lee of the rimrock, never blowing from the same quarter for more than a few minutes at a time. This meant that setting the adjustable smoke-flaps downwind was useless; no sooner were they set properly than the wind would gust from another direction. But the smoke-flaps were ingeniously contrived to alleviate that problem, too. The tops of the flaps were held higher than the apex of the tepee proper by two light poles that fitted into pockets sewn in the tips. By moving the butts of these poles around the tepee so the flaps faced downwind, a draft was created, drawing the smoke from the interior. Along the edges of these flaps were sewn two loose pieces of cloth. Normally they simply flapped in the breeze. But if the wind changed direction, these two loose pieces acted as valves, closing off the space between the flaps. Then, the flaps being higher than the apex of the tepee, the smoke was drawn out in the opposite direction!

My first experience with tepees was on a hunting trip up at the Top of the World. Our hunters were to sleep in the two tepees, and it fell to me to cut the twenty-six poles, each sixteen feet long, for the framework. At that elevation the trees were very scrubby. The only poles I could find were six inches or more on the butt end. I had to scrounge over half a square mile to find them and it took the greater part of the afternoon to collect and assemble them.

Not obtaining good poles could be a severe draw-back to the tepee. The Indians solved it by camping where good poles were readily available, leaving them in place, and using the same campground whenever possible. For my tepees, I had cut good jack pine poles down in the bottom lands where the tall, thin poles were plentiful. Then I'd hauled and packed them to wherever I intended my camps to be, and set them up to be used over and over. It meant a lot of hard work initially, but it paid off in the end. In the case of the camp Nataros and I had on the North Fork, I commandeered my sons to help, and we lugged the poles on our shoulders for miles up the mountain.

With the poles in place it was a quick and simple matter to pitch the tepee for each trip. I built the fire first and, while it was getting established, wrapped the tepee around it. On waking in the morning, without getting out of my sleeping bag I would reach out from a sitting position, kindle the fire in its rock fireplace from material prepared the night before, set the coffee pot on the edge of the rocks, and in ten minutes get up to a cozy, warm fire with hot coffee in the pot. If time permitted, we would have coffee in bed. Room service, tepee style.

The bottom edge of the tepee was never tight to the ground. Drafts, you say? Not so. Our sleeping bags were laid out on half of our groundsheet; the other half was stretched up the poles behind our beds and tied there. The draft was then channeled up between the outside cover and the ground sheet, never against our bodies. The Indians used to skirt the inside of the tepee completely, to about halfway up the poles. It was necessary to have a draft coming in the bottom and exiting through the smoke hole to carry the smoke out; otherwise, it would simply eddy within the tepee.

The tepee, then, was easily portable, light, quick to set up and dismantle, and tremendously efficient in a number of ways. The fact that the Indians used to live in them through the bitter winters on the borders of the Great Plains is a testimony to their worth.

When I finally sold out my guiding enterprise to Wally Faiers, my tepees were not included in the deal. No way would I part with them. Until, that is, our son Gary was stationed in Nova Scotia with the Air Force in 1966. To augment his Air Force pay he undertook to cut pulpwood for a farmer on his wood lot. He needed a shelter for refuge from the elements, so he borrowed my smaller tepee. It so happened that the farmer had a bull with very long horns. One hot summer day when the flies were bad, the bull decided to escape them by entering the tepee. He spent the afternoon tossing his head against the annoying flies. End of tepee number one. The other still lies in my basement. I haven't pitched it for many years, but perhaps one day I'll take it out to show our grandchildren how the Indians lived.

Grizzlies on the Bait

❖   ❖   ❖

BEAR-BAITING WAS STILL LEGAL in the early sixties. I didn't care for it on the grounds that it wasn't very sportsmanlike, but it was standard procedure with nearly all the guides. They, of course, had to produce for their clients or go out of business.

Actually, bear-baiting was not much different from hunting bears when they come down to the streams to feed on spawning salmon, a practice that is still common even in these enlightened times.

The Moyie country is in a heavy snow belt, with ten or fifteen feet falling in an ordinary winter. Bears coming out of hibernation in March or April are forced to come down from the high country to the creek bottoms, where the snow melts first, and find whatever sustenance they can. Since all hoofed game migrates down into the main Kootenay Valley in winter, there are no winter-kills for the bears to feed on. They have to do the best they can on a diet of early vegetation — the first tender shoots of grass and a few bulbs and roots.

Under these circumstances a protein bait, placed properly in a creek bottom just below the snow line, was irresistible. The bear population in the area was heavy at that time and was concentrated by spring conditions, so a bait all but assured the hunter's success.

The placing of the bait followed fairly standard procedures. First an elevation was chosen, a hillside or a knoll looking down on a small clear spot closely surrounded by brush, the thicker the better. This brush cover gave the bear a false sense of security while he fed. Bears never seem to realize that there may be danger from above.

The prevailing winds here blow from the west. In the absence of a general wind, the thermal breezes flow up the draw during the day and down during the night, with fitful breezes both up and down during the transition from warm to cool. Therefore the optimum location so far as wind is concerned is a north-south-striking draw with a blind, either constructed or natural, within a hundred yards or so of the selected clearing.

In the more remote areas, transporting bait to the site was simplified by using an old or infirm horse, or, rarely, a cow that was due to be put down. The animal could be led to the site and put down where it was needed.

An alternative, which I often used, was to collect a large amount of meat scraps and bones from the local butcher shops and transport them in boxes on a packboard. If a horse or cow was used, the carcass had to be chained to a stump, a large rock, or the bole of a tree to prevent the bear from dragging it out of the clearing. Bones and scraps avoided this problem by sheer weight of numbers. A bear might take a mouthful or two into the brush to eat it, but after a few trips back and forth he would simply lie down beside the heap and munch happily away.

Sportsmanlike or not, it was always a great thrill to see a grizzly come in on the bait, appearing to come out of nowhere, perhaps pawing the carcass over in a display of strength, nosing about, and finally settling down to dinner. Almost invariably the bear arrived during the hour before dark. The impending gloom, the silent white mountains in the background, patches of snow on the nearer hillsides, perhaps the yammering of a coyote in the distance, the brawling of the nearby creek, all lent an atmosphere that transported the human hunter back over thousands of years to the time when this was the way of life. To see a big silvertip appear, silently and unannounced, always caused the back hairs to bristle. A hunter seeing all this for the first time understandably developed a sudden case of the shakes.

It was late May, 1962. The bears would have come down from the high country, but their hides would still be good, and Frank Nataros wanted a bear. I knew the ideal spot for the bait, and in this instance I used a small, inbred cayuse that one of the horse-hunters was about to sell to a cannery for thirty-five dollars. I paid him that sum, the cayuse was spared the considerable trauma of being transported to the cannery, a friend of mine helped me with the little horse, and Frank was all but assured of a trophy.

It sometimes took several days for a bear to discover a bait. Frank, an optometrist in Claresholm, Alberta, was within easy driving distance of my headquarters in Cranbrook, so there was no need for him to lose time from his office. I had a job too, so I drove up the Moyie each evening after work to check things out. Since I would arrive late at the blind, the bears I saw were already at the kill when I came.

On my third visit I found that an old sow with twin cubs had moved in. Of course we were not about to shoot her. I retreated quietly and left her and the cubs to a free meal.

On the next evening I found that a good boar had
come in, no doubt having run off the sow and her family.
He was not a particularly large bear, but a fair trophy
nonetheless, so I went home and phoned Frank. He arrived
in Cranbrook the next afternoon. As soon as I finished my
work we drove quietly up an old logging road to a point
about half a mile from the blind and on the same level. I
always carried my own rifle when I had only one hunter in
grizzly country, just in case. We loaded our rifles, made the
sneak to the blind, and peeped hopefully down at the bait.

The boar I had seen the evening before was gone.
A much larger boar had run him off, and there he was, lying
broadside, feeding on the carcass.

I had guided Frank on two previous hunts, and I
knew him to be a cool head and a good shot. This was going
to be a piece of cake. He settled down behind the crossed
windfalls that constituted our blind, while I set up my
binoculars on the tripod. I was watching through the glasses
when Frank fired.

At the very instant Frank pulled the trigger, the
bear rose to his feet with a string of entrails in his mouth. We
heard the whump! of the bullet, but instead of floundering
as a bear would if struck solidly by a bullet from Frank's
.300 Weatherby Magnum, this bear wheeled and dived into
the brush.

Both Frank and I fired desperation shots as he
disappeared in the dense cover of lodgepole pine, but so few
and fleeting were the glimpses we had of him that our
efforts were futile. The lodgepole thicket extended more
than a mile down the creek, and for miles beyond that the
mountain terrain was a jumble of windfalls, willows, and
more lodgepole. Absolutely no chance of our ever seeing that
bear again, or so we thought.

It was soon apparent, however, that this bear had other things besides escape in mind. The small, slim trees, ten to fifteen feet tall, were as thick as they could stand, and we followed the bear's progress by the quaking of the treetops as he ran. He fled in a more or less straight line for a hundred yards or so, and then stopped. The agitation of the trees told us he was a very, very angry bear, and he was taking his anger out by flogging the brush. I doubted that he was badly hurt, judging by his quick action after Frank's first shot. He made no vocal sound, but those violently waving trees sent us a clear message: "Come and get me if you dare!"

Our shooting had given the bear all the information he needed, so we made no effort to be quiet.

"What do we do now?" Frank asked.

"Nothing we can do but go down there after him. He's too dangerous to leave wounded. We're not far from town, and someone else might come by. He'd attack them, sure as fate." There was that other moral dictum, too: never leave wounded game to suffer. If you're going to go around pot-shotting animals, you're duty-bound to see things through.

Even as we spoke there was fresh activity among the lodgepoles. Clearly the bear was not the least intimidated. When we went into that jungle after him, he would be able to pinpoint our progress by sound. He could cut and run, or ambush us, or stalk us, as he fancied. If we came to grips with him at all, it would be under conditions of his own choosing.

We had less than half an hour's shooting light left, and the prospect of being caught in the dark, in that already gloomy creek bottom, with an angry bear, was really scary. We could leave him until morning and return with reinforcement — but almost surely he would move during the night and roam the countryside, in a mood to attack and kill any casual passerby. No, we had to go after him, and now. At least there were two of us, and only one bear.

A rustle in the brush behind us made us turn around. There stood Ross Farquharson, the game warden, who had come to check out my operation, which of course was part of his job.

"That's quite a rifle you have there," he said, nodding at Frank. "I counted ten fast shots."

This was an oblique reference to the regulation which forbids a guide to shoot game for his client except under dire circumstances. Obviously all those shots couldn't have come from Frank's rifle. I explained quickly that the circumstances were dire, indeed, and the bear demonstrated my point by thrashing the trees vigorously again.

"We're going down after him," I said, "and I think it's going to be quite a show. I'm sure glad to see you. You can take the sad tidings back to our next-of-kin."

Ross was not amused. "Once you're down in that brush you won't be able to tell where he is. Do you think he's badly hurt?"

"No, I think he's just mad, and more concerned about keeping us away from the bait than anything else."

"Look," Ross said after sizing things up. "I know where he is, and from up here I can tell if he moves, and where you are. I'll stay here and direct you. Get a move on. It'll soon be dark. Be careful, and if it looks too bad, knock it off."

Frank and I checked our rifles once more and went down into the thicket. No use trying to keep quiet. The lodgepoles were so close we practically had to force our way through them, and small willows growing close to the ground made the going worse. Fortunately they hadn't leafed out yet, or our vision would have been even more restricted. A light thermal brought us a strong whiff of the ripening horse carcass, and if we needed anything more to impress us with the seriousness of our situation, that strong odor was it. That same thermal was carrying our scent to the bear.

Almost immediately Ross called out, "He's moving! There, he's stopped again. I think he hears you coming. Cut over a little to the left!"

We did so, and soon Ross called out again, "Watch out! I think he's laying for you! Thirty yards straight ahead!" And then, "He's a bad one! Twenty yards — be careful!"

I couldn't be sure whether Ross was putting us on a bit for Frank's benefit, but things were about as tense as they could get. If the bear really meant to challenge us, the moment of truth would come in the next couple of minutes. If he moved again we probably would have to abandon our effort, the light was failing so fast. And a nagging thought crossed my mind: if we began to withdraw, that might prompt him to attack.

Several times in my capacity as a guide I'd been involved in stalking previously made kills, in the hope of coming onto a bear feeding on the remains. To my mind that is the most thrilling situation a hunter can encounter. Only once had a hunter and I actually come upon a grizzly under those circumstances. The bear had charged, immediately and deliberately, and we'd been very lucky to come out of that one unscathed.

Another time my hunter and I had stumbled onto a grizzly cache with an old sow and two yearling cubs guarding it. My hunter had killed his bear the day before, so we had no wish to kill any of these. All three bears charged up the hill toward us. We ran back over the brow of the hill, cut sharply in behind a clump of brush, and held our breaths while the bears tore past.

Those had been sudden encounters, over before the full impact had time to register. This one had been going on for half an hour, with tension building all the while. Now, as I said, came the moment of truth.

Just ahead of us the lodgepoles seemed a bit thinner, the undergrowth a little less dense. I could see a big tamarack windfall some seventy feet from us, a logical ambush for the bear to choose, and I concentrated on that.

When we were fifty feet from the windfall I saw the bear's head pop up from behind it and duck back. We moved laterally to get a look down the length of the windfall before we got too close. The bear didn't wait. He poked his head up for another look, and this time gave Frank time for a shot.

End of drama. The bear collapsed behind the tamarack, shot through the brain, and congratulations were in order.

Ross helped us skin the bear in the failing light. The initial wound was worse than I had thought, low behind the rib cage, and for some reason the bullet had not exited. We couldn't take time for a postmortem, but obviously some internal organs had been damaged. The bear might have lived for some time, but death would have been the inevitable result.

Luckily the skull was not ruined for measurement, and Ross suggested that Frank enter it in the Boone and Crockett Club's *Records of North American Big Game*. Frank wrote to me some time later to say that the skull had indeed made the book, in 1964. It ranked in sixty-eighth place, a long way from the top. But with the typical silvertip guard hairs beautifully saddling the perfectly furred pelt, it was a trophy to be proud of, and the circumstances of its taking added immeasurably to Frank's satisfaction, and to mine.

Hunters and
Human Nature

❖   ❖   ❖

MY MOST SATISFYING TRIP on the Moyie was with a father-and-son team from the Midwest. The father was Richard, the son, Dick. The older man was in his late sixties, and like the Texan on an earlier hunt he had insisted on making the trip in spite of my objections. He was another of the hunters who disliked horses, and for that reason he was keen on what I offered. He had hunted each year for all of his adult life, but time was running out. This was to be his last trip.

His son, in his forties, was not the least bit interested in killing game. He had come with his father on the last hunt so they could be together doing what Richard loved best. It was touching to see the great regard they had for each other. I was determined to make this as satisfying for them as I possibly could. I took them up to some fairly open country on Lewisby Creek, where the going wasn't too rough.

The old man had killed a lot of game over the years, but three species had always eluded him. He offered me a ten percent bonus if he should collect an elk, a goat, and a grizzly.

On the third day we hunted along an old logging road on Ridgeway Creek. Our side of the valley was grown up in alders, but a good game trail ran along the road, so we could thread our way through the alders fairly easily. Below us the creek bottom was an open, grassy meadow. The opposing mountainside had been burned off cleanly, and there was unimpeded vision out to about five hundred yards.

Richard was packing a European-built 7x57 Mauser rifle that had a hunting scene engraved on the action, with a stag inlaid in gold. His scope mounts were quick-detachable and handcrafted. The front mount clamped into place with a small lever. When it was detached, the scope could be swung to the left ninety degrees, which disengaged the rear mount. It was the finest rifle-scope combination I have ever seen. For some reason I couldn't fathom, the old man carried the scope detached, in his hip pocket.

A three-point elk came out of the brush below us and started across the meadow. Richard engaged his scope, and his first shot broke the elk's front leg. That's when that old bugaboo, buck fever, took over. He emptied his rifle bang-bang-bang. He had brought only his magazine full of ammunition.

He took Dick's rifle, bang-bang-bang. The elk kept going, by now starting up the opposite slope. I handed him my own .270 Husqvarna. The third wild shot at a range of close to five hundred yards broke a hind leg. The elk was, of course, immobilized, and we hurried over for the coup de grace. We ended up with only one cartridge left among us. The old man shook all over for a long time.

The next day we went up the South Fork of the Moyie. There were many meadows along that stream, and the going was pretty good. Along about four o'clock in the afternoon we stopped for a rest in one of the meadows, and as a matter of course I began glassing the surrounding country. There was a goat bedded on the rimrock at the south end of the valley, and I pointed this out to the hunters.

He was much too far away for us to go after him that afternoon, but we watched him for a long while. He rose from his bed, browsed the bushes for a time, then wandered slowly down into a deep little brushy draw to one side. I thought there probably was a spring in the draw, and the goat was going for water. Shortly he reappeared and continued browsing for as long as we watched.

On the opposite side of the spring was an over-hanging cliff. It angled down the mountain almost to the bottom, and it was too sheer for even a goat to climb. There was a possibility that the goat was following a set pattern of behavior, and just might repeat the same performance the next day. It would be too hard a climb for Richard to make it up to where the goat was bedded, but if I could get the hunters into an ambush at the foot of that cliff, I might be able to circle up the mountain behind the goat and drive him down along the cliff into the range of Richard's 7-mm rifle.

We were up early the next morning, and by noon we had reached the meadow from where we had seen the goat. He was bedded in much the same position as he had been. Keeping to the timber, we worked our way to the spot where I intended to leave the hunters in ambush. A peek through the trees told us that the goat was still in his bed.

Hurrying as fast as I could, I made a big circle up the mountain to get behind and above the goat. I had nearly reached the point where I should start the drive, when there were two shots from below. There was nothing for it but to go back down and check on the meaning of those two shots. Either they had killed him or he was long gone.

"He came right out on that little bench and looked right down at us," Richard said, pointing, when I reached them.

"Did you hit him?"

Dick answered. "I was watching through my binoculars when Dad shot," he said. "I saw wool fly after both shots."

"Stay here," I directed, "while I go up and have a look. Guide me by hand signals so I can find exactly where he was when you shot."

It was about 150 yards to where the goat had been. There was no blood in evidence, but then a goat, being such a woolly creature, seldom leaves a blood trail. I picked up his tracks and followed them back another hundred yards, where I found him dead. I fired a shot in the air and shouted that I had found him. To my surprise, Richard beat Dick up to me. It was amazing what a burst of vitality the old man showed.

The goat was a very fine specimen, with horns measuring just a trifle over ten inches. His early fall pelage was in fine condition, and he would make an interesting mount.

On the way back down the mountain with my heavy burden I made a detour to avoid a particularly steep, windfall-infested section. The two hunters took the shorter way down, and when I caught up to them the first thing I noticed was that Richard's scope was missing from his hip pocket. Neither was it on his rifle. Being handcrafted, the mating mounts were going to be awfully hard to duplicate. Since there was no mass production, new parts could not be bought off the shelf. The loss of the scope was less important than the loss of the mount parts.

I went back up to where we had dressed the goat

and began searching. It looked hopeless. There was much small brush on the ground, and I would nearly have to step on the scope before I found it. Then, too, the hunters had taken a different route, I had to track them as well as keep my eye peeled for the scope.

I found where they had crossed over a waist-high windfall, and there lay the scope! Richard had slid over the log on his butt and wiped the scope out of his pocket. Jubilation!

On the way back to the truck I made a detour to where my previous party had killed a moose. A grizzly had found it and buried the remains after he had fed. The kill was on the edge of a meadow through which a small stream meandered. Opposite the meadow from the kill was a broad game trail. Often a grizzly will bury a find like that and not come back for a long time. It looked as though this bear had buried the remains some days previously, and there was a chance that he might come back one evening soon.

The next morning I packed out the rest of the goat, giving Richard a chance to rest. The excitement and effort had just about done him in. But late in the afternoon we were sitting along the game trail across from the moose kill. If our luck held, Richard was going to get his grizzly and I was going to collect that ten percent bonus.

We sat quietly waiting. The air was calm and the deciduous foliage was bright with color. Away off on the ridge behind us a coyote started his evening yammering. The little creek in front of us gurgled pleasantly. It was a fine evening, and bear or no bear, we were all enjoying it immensely.

Suddenly in the brush along the trail just below us, all hell broke loose. An elephant couldn't have made more noise. A beautiful dark grizzly, his silver guard hairs rippling with every jump, landed in the middle of the creek with a tremendous splash. In the wink of an eye he crossed the little meadow and disappeared in the brush on the opposite slope. It all happened so quickly that Richard didn't have time to get in a shot. Undoubtedly the bear had smelled our tracks when he crossed the trail, and promptly bolted. Had he come in above us I would surely have collected my bonus.

No matter. It had been my best hunt ever, not because of the game we had collected, but because of the immense satisfaction the men had enjoyed.

The next summer I had a phone call one evening. The two were in Cranbrook, not on a hunt, but just to visit the country where they had had such an enjoyable time. Would Alta and I care for a steak dinner? The best Cranbrook had to offer? We would.

A big-game guide has to be more than just a good hunter; he also needs to know something about human nature. One of my parties was supposed to be two men from Arkansas. When they arrived in Cranbrook I discovered to my dismay that they had brought their wives with them. The idea was that the ladies were to stay in a motel in town while the men did their thing in the Great Outdoors.

Ten days in a motel in Cranbrook without knowing a soul? Impossible. But I could see the potential for some pleasure for the women and a little extra loot for me. I made a phone call, then struck a deal with my clients that not only made money for Alta and me, but saved it for them.

Bill Smith owned two nice cabins on Weaver Creek, where he had a placer gold lease. That was what the phone call was about. I rented the cabins for five dollars a day. Alta wangled a couple of weeks vacation from her job at Scott National. She would cook for the expedition and baby-sit the two ladies. Baby-sitting consisted of day trips to such exotic places as Old Town, Historic Fort Steele, the fish hatchery at Bull River, and Fairmont Hot Springs. They picked huckleberries for a couple of days, and Alta showed them heaps of bear dung, pointing out which ones she thought were black bear and which were grizzly. The ladies were thrilled.

Not so the men. My original plans had called for a tepee camp away back near the headwaters of the Moyie, but the advent of the wives changed the picture. There wasn't much game down on Weaver Creek at that time of year, the weather was hot and dry, and I couldn't even show the men a fresh track, much less a legal animal. By the end of the third day they were muttering darkly about going home to hunt rabbits.

It was possible to find a little fine gold in the gravel bars on Negro Creek. The fourth morning I tossed a couple of gold pans and a shovel into the back of the pickup and announced that we would hunt that day on Negro Creek.

What a change! Those two men spent the next three days mucking around in the creek raising blisters on their hands while I lolled on the bank and brewed coffee. Then it rained and the weather turned cool. We killed two grizzlies and a moose one day, and another moose the next. They went back to Arkansas with their trophies and a couple of dollars' worth of gold in their little bottles. I daresay those bottles are still sitting on their mantelpieces right below the mounted heads.

❖   ❖   ❖

My most successful party bagged a caribou, a black bear, two moose, and two grizzlies in five days. The next year, this party hunted in Alaska, a pack trip complete with horses, a wrangler, and a guide for each hunter — the whole bit. They phoned me the next summer and booked with me again for the fall. Alaska, they said, was for the birds.

Inevitably the time came when I guided my last party. They were four men from Seattle, and they wanted nothing but moose. They killed two moose, all right, and on the final evening of the ten-day hunt they settled up with me. They laid out sixteen hundred dollars in twenty-dollar bills on the table. I had never seen so much money in one pile in all my life.

I paid Alta twenty dollars a day for cooking, and the same for John Avis as assistant guide. The only other expenses had been a barrel of gas that was only half used, and perhaps a hundred dollars in groceries. Meat was free, and the vegetables came from our own garden. I cleared a little more than a thousand dollars for the trip, which was a lot of loot in those days, when a laborer's wages were fifteen to twenty dollars a day.

Those Seattle hunters had killed only two moose in the ten days, and I felt I owed them a little more. Alta and I decided to throw a party for them. We had stayed in the Weaver Creek cabins for that hunt. When Alta went to work at Scott National that last day, she invited some of the staff to come up to the cabins that night. I played the violin and a couple of the guests played banjo and guitar.

Along about eight o'clock that evening our guests began to arrive. In no time things began to shape up. We drank and sang and danced polkas on the rough plank floor for a couple of hours.

One of the town guests was a petite French girl. The hunters, of course, had been celibate for some time. The alcohol they consumed didn't help matters when it hit their hot blood. About two o'clock in the morning the little French girl decided to dance on top of the big kitchen range. One of the boys just couldn't restrain himself. He started chasing the girl around the cabin.

She ran out through the door, looking back and tossing her curls as she went onto the big porch. The hunter ran after her. It was dark out there. He saw her making for the corner of the cabin, and he ran to head her off. There was a great big wood box out there that held nearly a rick of stove wood, but at the time was empty.

We all heard the crash. We rushed out with the gas lantern and found the hunter just climbing from the box. Fortunately he sustained only two barked shins. The girl escaped.

We wound the party up at 5:00 A.M. with a pancake breakfast. Probably those hunters have long forgotten the details of bagging their moose, but I'll wager they still remember the lively little party we held in the cabin on Weaver Creek.

My father had a saying, "If it rained soup a poor man wouldn't have a spoon." The next year I booked two ten-day parties in addition to the Nataros brothers. When I asked my boss for time off he said no; he was sorry, but adamant. I could see his point. The business we ran at the Co-op was very complicated. It just wasn't possible to pick a man from the street who could handle the job. A clerk had to put in at least a full year to get a working knowledge through the changing seasons, each with its own peculiarity.

"Sorry, Fee," he said. "You'll have to do one or the other, either work here or go to guiding."

It was a temptation. But there were signs that times were changing on the Moyie. New roads had been built, and more were in prospect. In another year or two the whole area would be open to local hunters. Already they had discovered the potential for bears, and in the spring there were several bear baits set up along the roads. One spring evening my hunters took two grizzlies. The following evening two more were killed by local hunters. The bear population just couldn't stand that kind of pressure.

The Moose Pasture had been discovered and cleaned out. The little band of goats in the Moyie canyon were wiped out, although I hadn't taken any since the Nataros brothers' first trip. Loss of habitat was having its effect on the caribou. Then, too, the season was too short for a full-time vocation. I sold out to Wally Faiers for the grand sum of one thousand dollars, and I took two hundred of that in trade, an old beat-up Studebaker car.

"If it rained soup a poor man wouldn't have a spoon." I saw what Pa meant. The party for the Seattle hunters was a fitting climax to my days on the Moyie. The whole venture had been extremely interesting and satisfying, and I had proved a point: that it was not necessary to have a string of horses to carry out a successful guiding business. I had found that there were many people who had a dislike of horses. And I found, too, that there were many people who could not afford a full-scale pack trip, but could take advantage of my prices and hunt for what to them was exotic game. Aside from one short trip when I guided with Wally as assistant, I never hunted the Moyie again.

V

❖ ❖ ❖

REFLECTIONS

Many Waters

❖   ❖   ❖

MANY WATERS CAMPGROUND was located on Wild Horse Creek just above the seventeen-mile post on the present logging road. The big-game guides, who camped there with their hunters in the fall, gave the spot its name. A variety of trophy animals abounded in the area before the advent of the loggers.

The name, as was often the case with early-day place-names, was both colorful and descriptive. Several small springs bubbled from the ground. A small creek rippled in from a series of high alpine basins to the east. Just a short stone's throw to the west and barely below the level of the camp flowed the waters of Wild Horse Creek. The creek bottom and the mountain slopes were covered with a heavy stand of virgin timber, mostly spruce and balsam, giving off the typical sweet odor of the high country. Above the timber rose the peaks of the Hughes Range of the Rocky Mountains, with their beautiful cirques and meadows. The two creeks and the many springs, along with tent spaces and a holding corral for horses, took up an area of less than an acre.

One of the springs produced warm water. It was

called a hot spring, though the water was barely more than skin temperature. Someone, probably Indians long before the arrival of the white man, had dug out a hole with the spring in the center, forming a bowl perhaps six feet in diameter and three or four feet deep, rimmed with the displaced material. The water boiled up from a hole in the center with considerable force, a perfect, natural whirlpool bath. Many a weary mountaineer had bathed his aching muscles in the soothing waters after a hard day's climbing in the peaks.

The only access was by pack trail. Those few who were fortunate enough to have camped in that beautiful, secluded spot did so in the belief that it would ever remain so. A formidable canyon a few miles down the creek posed an insurmountable obstacle to the builders of roads — or so they thought.

One of the guides who used the camp periodically was Harry Bjorn, now retired and living on his farm on Skookumchuck Prairie. Harry thought it would be fitting to erect a sign welcoming wilderness travelers to the camp, and so he carved a sign on whip-sawed slabs, saying "Welcome to Many Waters," and nailed it to a tree.

But as the years passed, the timber in the valley became more and more valuable. Logging technology improved. And so a road was blasted and bulldozed through the "impassable" canyon, and the doom of Many Waters was sealed.

Several years ago an old-timer who had camped there many times in the past came to camp again. He found the area a complete wasteland, bulldozed beyond recognition. The virgin timber of the creek bottom and moutainsides was virgin no more.

He found the tree to which the sign had been nailed

— uprooted. The sign lay there, its face to the sky like a sightless corpse. The old-timer felt as though the bulldozer had run over his heart.

The thought came to mind that Harry might like to have the sign as a memento of younger days. Or would he? Under the circumstances, probably not. The old man lugged the sign home, where it has lain in his backyard in Cranbrook for many years, a symbol of the changing times.

The old man called the local Forestry Department to report the desecration of the campground. He was told that it was necessary to clear out all the timber because it was "infested with bugs." The Forestry official didn't explain why a small thicket of spruce trees less than fifty yards from the hot springs, a thicket that held no useful timber, had been left. Perhaps close inspection revealed that there were no "bugs" in that particular stand?

"Welcome to Many Waters," indeed!

Just Like a Park

❖   ❖   ❖

"IT'S JUST LIKE A PARK UP THERE," the Great White Hunter said to Frank, motioning with his hands to indicate a gentle slope. "There's three inches of snow on the grass. Two of us could put a rope on the elk and skid him right to the edge of the mountain, dump him over, and be back down to the road in an hour."

Teresia and Frank had stopped to visit the hunter where he was camped in a little log cabin halfway up a mountain just southeast of Canal Flats. The hunter had killed a spike elk earlier in the day, up on top of the mountain, and he was trying to talk Frank into coming back in the morning to help bring it out. Frank was wary. He and the hunter both worked in the Sullivan Mine, and ever since the time they had been working forty feet up a ladder, and the hunter had dropped a big ball peen hammer on Frank's head, Frank avoided getting involved with him any more than he could help. The guy was accident prone.

The hunter's companion (we'll call him the gun-bearer) sat quietly in a corner of the shack nursing a bottle of beer. A nearly full bottle of rye sat on the table. Stew in a long-handled saucepan bubbled niccly on the rounded top of a big barrel heater, giving off a delicious odor. A Coleman gas lantern hissed quietly where it hung from a hook in the ceiling.

"Yes, sir," the hunter said again, "it's beautiful up there. Just like a park."

He reached down for a bottle of beer standing in the sand-filled box that fireproofed the floor from the heater. The bottle had tipped over against the hot stove and absorbed considerable heat. It burned the hunter's hand. He jumped up, flinging the hot bottle across the room, swearing as he did so.

Teresia, always prepared for any eventuality, rushed out to their truck and came back with a big jar of Noxema ointment, with which she anointed the hunter's burned hand. He, still muttering obscenities, opened another bottle and set it back down in the sandbox, giving the stew a stir as he did so.

After a little conversation he bent over to reach for the beer. As his head went down his forehead struck the projecting handle of the saucepan. The pan rolled off the rounded top of the stove and turned neatly upside down on the hunter's head. Boiling stew poured down the tender spots behind his ears to his shirt collar. Teresia was there in a flash, wiping the hot stew off his head with one hand, slathering on Noxema with the other. He was lucky. He suffered only one blister the size of a quarter behind one ear, thanks to Teresia's quick action.

She said later that he sure looked funny with all that white ointment in his hair.

Frank phoned me that night. "Want half an elk?"

"Sure. What's the catch?"

He clued me in on the situation. It seemed that the gunbearer wasn't in shape physically to help bring the elk out, but Teresia and Frank's son, Lorne, was willing to help if I would go along. "But I'm warning you to watch out while that guy's around. He's simply unbelievable!" He told me about the hot bottle, the stew, and the ball peen hammer.

Lorne and I were up at the cabin early the next morning. The hunter and the gunbearer were still in bed. An empty rye bottle stood on the table. Both men appeared very shaky when they crawled out of their sleeping bags. Neither wanted breakfast.

"You won't need your lunches or packboards," the hunter assured us, blinking bloodshot eyes. "We'll be back here by noon. But you better take your rifles. There were fresh grizzly tracks in the snow up there yesterday. It'll be easy to get the elk out. It's just like a park."

The sky was overcast, but the snow was starting to melt. In an hour we had climbed by a roundabout route to the top of the mountain where the elk lay. We crossed the trail of a hunting cougar and also the grizzly tracks the hunter had mentioned. We had passed over some rock ledges through a series of small cliffs, and the hunter assured us that the easiest way to get the elk down was over the brow of the mountain to the west, where the going would be much easier.

It was just like a park, all right, with three inches of snow on the grass, and on a gentle slope. Trouble was, the slope ran in the wrong direction. The hunter was the only one of us who had a packboard. He had a forty-foot length of skinny nylon rope on it. I had a length wrapped around my waist. We tied the ropes on the elk, gave the gunbearer our rifles to carry, and the rest of us leaned into the ropes. It was all the three of us could do to move the stiffened carcass up the slope toward the drop-off to the valley below.

It took us half an hour to skid the elk to the edge,

and there we were confronted with a steep, brush-choked gully. If the elk ever got into the bottom of that ravine we would have to stay there and eat the thing. Lorne pointed down into the draw. "Just like a park," he muttered in disgust.

We had to drag the elk across the slope to the head of the draw. Gravity constantly made the elk's body want to take the direct route to the bottom. We came to a rock slide consisting of big boulders, and in one place a huge, slick tamarack windfall lay directly up and down the slide. With Lorne and the hunter pulling hard on the ropes and me boosting the elk from behind, we got the carcass up onto the windfall lying balanced on its belly. I had to cross the windfall below the elk to rejoin the others, and I stepped carefully up onto the greasy wood. That's when I got a demonstration of what Frank had told me. The hunter shouted impatiently, "Let's go!" and gave a tug on the rope. The elk shot down the windfall, straight toward my feet. I had no alternative but to jump into the jumble of big boulders, and how I avoided falling, perhaps breaking a leg, is anybody's guess. Lorne was aghast at my close call, but the hunter and the gunbearer both reacted as though it was all in a day's work.

We were lucky we had two ropes. One man anchored up the hill, while two of us tugged mightily to get the carcass across inch by inch. Eventually we managed to circumvent the worst part. We crossed the draw to the top of the next low ridge and had good going down to the bench below. By this time the carcass had limbered up, and bare patches of hide were showing where the hair had been worn off.

The overcast had lowered and tendrils of fog were swirling around our heads, but still we could see down to the bottom of the mountain. It was a long way down. The gunbearer was hanging back a hundred yards or so and was having a hard time. I could sympathize with him; anyone could who had ever tried carrying four rifles over rough terrain. It was past noon, and both Lorne and I were getting mighty hungry. The other two, with no breakfast and hung over to boot, must have been still worse off.

The bench we were now on was about 150 feet wide. Oddly, at that altitude, it held a long, narrow slough that was covered with ice and snow.

"Hope the ice is strong enough to hold us," I said. "Otherwise we'll have to drag this thing around it through the brush."

"Oh, no problem," the hunter replied confidently. "It's been cold enough. It'll be frozen solid," and he stepped briskly out onto it. The ice was about a quarter of an inch thick. The water was only a couple of inches deep, but in an instant the hunter was up to his hips in white alkali mud. Just in front of him was a small, grassy hummock like a little island with a good-sized willow growing on it. With a great churning of mud he fought his way to it. He emerged dripping mud and water. "Man, but that's cold!" he said.

It was a long jump back to solid land. He squatted down for the effort. Just before he leaped I could see what was going to happen, but he ignored my shout of warning. One stout trunk of the willow leaned just above his head. When he leaped the willow fitted nicely between his head and the packboard, making him flip backward and come down on his back with a great splash. Try as he might, the springy willow resisted his efforts to remove it, and he sat struggling with it for the better part of a minute before he finally worked free, all the while churning his feet desperately to keep afloat.

Lorne and I were hysterical with laughter. The gunbearer simply stood with a bemused expression on his face. Apparently this was normal behavior, nothing to laugh about.

It took more than another hour of savage effort before we cleared the end of the slough, only to find ourselves on the edge of a precipice thirty feet high. No problem here, simply dump the elk over the edge.

"No, no!" the hunter objected. "I want steak, not hamburger!" We had pulled the carcass right to the edge of the cliff. A stout little fir tree grew there. Lorne pointed out that we could take a turn or two around it with the ropes and lower the elk down gently. The hunter decided not to take the turn. Holding the rope alone, with it bearing only against the side of the tree, he reached out with his foot and shoved the elk over the brink. I thought there was no way he was going to hold it from falling, but no matter. He was just going to have to be content with hamburger.

He had a big tangle of rope on the ground behind him. When the elk dropped, the rope zipped through his hands. The tangle just jumped into the air and snagged on one of the hooks on his packboard. The packboard came up against the back of his head and yanked him hard against the tree. It looked as though he were going to be dragged around the tree and down over the cliff along with the elk.

His guardian angel must have been hovering close by. For some reason the elk stopped falling. Quickly Lorne and I untangled the hunter and snubbed the rope. A look over the edge revealed that there was a big fissure in the rock face below, and the elk had jammed in it at the last possible moment!

We managed to free the elk with the second rope, which was still attached, and lower it gently as should have been done in the first place. Then we found ourselves on another broad ledge, and there was another cliff below us. Not far from the bottom of this one we could see the road. That was our last hurdle. There was nothing to anchor to, so we kicked the elk over and heard it crash on the talus below. The cliff ran for a considerable distance in either direction, and we had to look for a way down. We came to a cleft, an almost vertical chimney running down the face. It twisted around a bulge in the rock and we couldn't see the bottom.

"I've been here before," the hunter said. "We can get down here easy." He started backing down the chimney, and we watched him disappear around the bulge. Suddenly there was the clatter of falling rock. Boulders bounded down into the trees below. This had to be the end of the Great White Hunter!

We stood looking down the chimney, horrified at this last calamity. But no! Around the bulge of rock came a red cap, followed by the hunter. He turned a white face up to us. "No," he shouted, "we can't get down this way either!"

Enough was enough. We were all trembling with hunger and exhaustion. "That's it!" Lorne said decisively. "We're going back to the cabin. We'll come back and get the elk tomorrow!" the gunbearer, in particular, seemed to be in bad shape. His face was pale and drawn, and he was having trouble breathing.

When we reached the cabin the two packed up their belongings and headed for town. The next day the hunter returned for the elk, which was now on a nice parklike slope just above the road. Lorne and I declined to help him. The gunbearer didn't accompany him either. He had died of a heart attack during the night.

Odd as it may seem, the hunter is still around, in good health and spirits, although he is still performing his strange antics. The last time I saw him we were parked on the other side of a three-foot ditch beside the highway when he came down the road at good speed. His boat was on top of the car, so evidently he had been fishing at some nearby lake. When he saw us he applied the brakes, whipped the steering wheel over, and turned straight for the ditch. His speed was such that the front wheels of the car cleared the ditch, but the hind wheels came down short with a sickening crunch. The ropes holding the boat on the car broke, and the boat flew over the hood of the car, the bow digging deep in the dirt.

At least this time he scared himself. He was slow getting out of the car, and we thought he had been hurt. But when he finally emerged we saw that he had only wet his pants.

How Come?

❖   ❖   ❖

"HOW COME YOU NEED a new tire?" Wendell Dempsey asked. "Blowout?"

"No, not exactly," Jack answered, grinning. "Actually, a bear ruined it."

Before he could get into the story, his wife, Joan, started snickering, and in a moment both of them were rocking with laughter.

"What did the bear do? Bite a hole in your tire?" Wendell's wife, Emma, asked when the hilarity had subsided.

"No, it was like this. . . ."

The story sounded incredible. But the way the two traded the narration back and forth it was obvious that they could not have made it up without an awful lot of rehearsing, and when Wendell finally saw the tire he knew the story had to be true.

Emma and Wendell Dempsey were operating the old Kershaw store at Fort Steele, British Columbia. Fort Steele is one of the oldest communities in the southeastern part of the province. In the late 1800s, when the railroad was coming through, Fort Steele was intended to be the hub of

commerce in the East Kootenay District. But politics entered
the picture, the railway bypassed the town, and the commu-
nity declined to barely more than a ghost town. Today it is
world-famous as Fort Steele Historic Park.

The Dempseys sold the usual assortment of groceries
found in a small country store, along with a bit of hardware
and gasoline. They kept the business much as it had been
through the years, and many a stranger found it intriguing.
Naturally they had a number of good local stories to tell
to those who had the time and inclination to listen. This
is the gem of them all.

It was a morning in early May when Jack and Joan
asked Wendell to drive them to Cranbrook, ten miles away,
so they could buy a new tire. They had been in the store
several times during the spring, and the Dempseys were
getting to know them well.

They were professional prospectors. They traveled
wherever their fancy led, mining various creeks and bars
for placer gold. They had prospected in Alaska, the Yukon,
the Cariboo, and many other exotic places, never making a
big strike but gleaning enough of the precious yellow metal
to meet their few needs. They had no responsibilities other
than to themselves, and they were enjoying a wonderful
gypsy way of life.

Their traveling home was a big, old, beat-up panel
truck. Their few possessions were mainly tools of their trade,
such as picks, shovels, a mattock, gold pan, hip waders for
working in the cold waters of the chosen creeks, a good ax,
a rifle, and a sluice box. Their clothing was of the workman's
variety, worn but clean. They wore high-quality logger's
boots, well-greased and comfortable. The term "sourdough"
described them well.

With them they had a big black pup. When he got

his full growth he would be a powerful dog, ideal for packing. He was happily adjusting to their way of life, enjoying each new lesson immensely.

Their peregrinations had led them to the old Wild Horse diggings, where gold estimated at twenty-five million dollars (at eighteen dollars an ounce) had been taken out of four and a half miles of creek bed back in the period 1864 to 1878. It is interesting to note that most of this gold was taken out by American miners. The gold went to the San Francisco Mint, and helped strengthen the American economy following the Civil War. Fisherville was the gold camp of the day, but it had long since disappeared. Fort Steele, itself on the verge of decay, was the nearest store and post office.

The young couple had been working a likely looking gulch up on the creek for some time, with little success. There were still pockets of gold to be found in places, but not nearly as rich as in the old days. On a good, hard day of sluicing, they would make expenses and a little more. And some days would turn up a good nugget or two, naturally raising hopes and spurring effort.

The snow had gone at the lower elevations, but when the heavy pack at the upper levels started melting the resultant high water had flooded out their workings. They decided to move on, possibly to the Nevada goldfields or even California. Accordingly they packed their tools down from the gulch and loaded them into the truck. They had a mattress on the floor, and they piled their equipment on it. The sluice box was too long for the body of the panel, so they had to leave the back doors open with a red rag tied to the projecting end of the box. On top of the tools they placed their sleeping bags, cooking utensils, and grub box.

They had gone a short distance down the rough Wild Horse road when one of their tires blew. Not to worry. In short order they had replaced it with their spare. By the time they had negotiated the ten miles down to the highway near Fort Steele it was getting late in the day. They decided to camp for the night on a nice, level gravel bar beside the highway bridge. Rather than unload all their equipment down to the mattress, they thought it better to sleep sitting up on the seat of the vehicle, wrapped individually in their eiderdown sleeping bags.

They cooked a good meal, washed the dishes, and sat for a time watching the dying embers of the fire and the fading light on the magnificent Rockies to the east. The sound of the brawling creek and the fragrance of the early growing things added to their euphoria.

But they'd had a hard day and were tired. Time to go to bed. The creek bottom was a likely place for skunks, porcupines, and assorted other mischievous creatures, so to avoid nighttime disturbance the pup would have to sleep with them in the panel — a development much to his liking. Normally he slept outside.

Shortly they were asleep, the pup curled up between them, Jack's rifle with magazine loaded, muzzle down on the floor, butt leaning against the seat. It had been a good day, as most of their days were.

In the dark middle hours of the night a black bear came slowly out of the willows flanking the gravel bar. He made out the form of the truck close by, and his curiosity was aroused. He didn't like the smell of gas, oil, and rubber. There was another scent, too, which caused him to pause — the scent of human beings. Way back in dim memory he had dared to enter a cabin, where the same smell was rank. That time the rewards had been great.

Cautiously he approached the open back of the truck. He rose to his hind feet, resting one forepaw lightly on the projecting sluice box. The tantalizing smell of bologna came to his nostrils. As gently as possible he eased his big bulk into the open rear doors, carefully inching inside. Soon he located the source of the rich scent, a grub box with the lid open just a fraction.

A tin water pail balancing restlessly on its edge tipped over with a tiny clink. The bear froze. In the unaccustomed confinement of the truck he was very nervous.

Jack awoke. His position was uncomfortable, and he shifted on the seat. He yawned a couple of times and drifted back to the edge of sleep. Suddenly he felt a queer sensation. Whether it was dream or reality, he wasn't sure, but it brought him back to wakefulness. It seemed as though the back of the truck had sagged way down. Queer, indeed!

The next couple of minutes were to be the most terrifying moments any of the company present — Jack, Joan, the pup, and the bear — had ever endured.

Jack heard the clink of the water pail from the cavern behind him. He turned his head. Looming black even in the darkness was the form of a large bear!

"*Bear!*" Jack shouted, thrusting his body heavily against the sleeping pup.

The pup, awakened so rudely by this rough action, smelled the odor of bear in his nostrils and yelped loudly, recoiling against Joan.

Joan, awakened from deep slumber, thought she had been attacked. Sleeping bag and all, she scrambled over the top of the seat into the back — with the bear.

The bear had been temporarily paralyzed with fear by Jack's shout — the most blood-curdling sound he had ever heard. But when Joan came hurtling over the seat at him, he recovered his senses and flew out the back of the truck in a tremendous leap.

Jack felt the truck lurch, but he thought it was the bear pouncing on his wife. Frantically he fought one arm free of the sleeping bag and grasped his rifle. The frightened pup tried to climb onto his lap. The rifle was too long to turn in the confined space, and Jack couldn't get the muzzle over the back of the seat. It was just as well, since the only living thing back there was his wife.

In the struggle with the pup, the gun butt hit the door handle. The door flew open, and Jack fell out backward onto the gravel. The pup fell out too, and with tail tucked tightly against him he fled across the highway bridge, yelping as he went.

Joan came fully awake just in time to see the bear depart, but she didn't know where he had gone. She scrambled back onto the seat she had so recently vacated. The door was open and her husband was gone. There seemed to be a scuffle going on out in the gravel, and she heard the pup yelping. She didn't know what to do, so she just cowered back on the seat, staring out into the darkness.

The bear, meanwhile, ran desperately through the willows, heading north up the creek.

Completely addled now, his senses dulled by the rough contact with the ground, Jack managed to get back onto his feet. As far as he knew, the bear was mauling his wife in the back of the truck. His upper body was finally free of the sleeping bag, but he didn't realize he was still standing in the folds. He lurched for the door, chambering a cartridge in the rifle. The sleeping bag tripped him up, and he fell. The rifle hit the ground and discharged. Fire spurted from the muzzle, directly toward the left hind wheel of the vehicle. Ka-*boom*! The smell of burnt gun-powder, dust, and hot rubber filled the night air.

That's how come they needed a new tire.

Other Dimensions

❖   ❖   ❖

BECAUSE I LOOK AT LIFE with humor, I have often interpreted situations amongst wildlife as revealing this trait. I think that the raven, perhaps more than any other wild creature, shows a fine sense of humor. And the bumbling black bear is the perfect fall guy.

This was borne out one October day, one of those glorious Indian summer days of which I am so fond. I was hunting up on Kishaneena Creek. Hunting is not the proper word. I had killed a moose the week before, so my thoughts were not on adding to the score but just enjoying the sights, sounds, and smells of the high country.

I was walking on an old road that crossed a slide — an avalanche path — when I noticed what appeared to be a big black stump way up on the mountain. But of course there would not be a stump that big out on an open slide, especially at that elevation. My binoculars confirmed what I already suspected. It was an unusually big black bear.

I had no particular wish to shoot another bear, but the money paid for a good hide was something to consider. Still, my conscience told me that there was no real reason other than money to end the animal's life. Besides, it was a long way up to him, and possibly by the time I had made the climb he would be long gone, or he wouldn't prove to be such an outstanding specimen after all. And then there would be the inevitable job afterward.

While I was mulling it over the issue was decided in a way that gave me far more pleasure than the killing of the bear could ever do. Into the field of view of my binoculars and far above the bear, a lone raven came winging. When he cleared the peak of the mountain and saw the bear, he closed his wings and peeled into an almost vertical dive straight for the animal. That was surprising. Why would a raven attack an animal that large?

The raven pulled out of his dive just a few feet above the victim. At once his intention was clear. The bear of course had no inkling of the raven's presence. When the bird braked, the rush of air through his wings must have set up quite a noise, which I couldn't hear because of the distance.

The bear was galvanized into instant action. Not knowing the source of the weird noise, and scared out of his wits, he fled at top speed for the nearest cover, a dense thicket of jack pine a hundred yards below. The raven wheeled sharply, towered, and buzzed him twice more before the bear reached cover. I could only think, from the speed he was going when he entered the timber, that he must have suffered many bruises. The raven flew on across the valley, and by his jaunty manner it was plain that he was sensing the satisfaction of a practical joker who had pulled off a successful prank.

Two of the most fascinating hours of my life came on a hot summer's day when I was scouting out a new part of my guiding territory on the Moyie River. I had camped for the night at the foot of a high, bare ridge that runs from the North Fork of the Moyie to the headwaters of Perry Creek. After an early start in the morning I was making my way along the top of the ridge at about ten o'clock. I came over a steep bit of rimrock to see a gaunt old female grizzly just below me. She hadn't shed all of her winter pelage, and a great clump of matted hair hung down behind her haunches. With her were two little blond cubs, each about the size of a small water spaniel.

Just below where I was standing was a ledge on the side of a forty-foot cliff. I eased my way down onto the ledge and set up my 10x50 binoculars on the low tripod I carried. The bears were less than a hundred yards away, and through the ten-power glasses they appeared to be only thirty or forty feet distant. The old sow had a good escape route open to her and the cubs, so there was no danger that she would attack me should she discover I was there.

The day was brilliant, the only wind was the thermal breeze that flowed up the hill, so it was unlikely the old girl would get my scent. The mossy ledge was shaded by a tall clump of trees, and I relaxed there on my belly quietly watching the performances of the little family.

The sow had dug several excavations on the steep side of the ridge, each one big enough to hold a kitchen range. She had just completed one when I came on the scene. The soil she had excavated lay in a pile. She nosed over the heap, licking up small goodies that I couldn't identify even through the powerful binoculars. After having worked over the surface of the dirt pile she very daintily brushed over it with her huge paw, revealing another layer which she then ran over with lips and tongue. Then another layer, and another, until she had reduced the pile completely. She then moved a few feet and, arching her big claws and bunching her shoulders, dug out another hole where she repeated the whole performance. Whatever she was feeding on must have been tasty; certainly she was not getting enough sustenance to repay the expenditure of energy.

While mother was occupied thus, the cubs wrestled and scuffled in play. The slope was steep, and invariably when they clinched and rolled they tumbled down the hill like furry balls until they came up against some obstruction. Then they would break, regain their feet, and scramble back up to the sow. They played so hard and kept at it so long that they seemed to be on the verge of exhaustion, their little pink tongues hanging out as they panted. It seemed that mother paid them no heed, and one would be led to wonder whether she was a very good mother to them.

After half an hour or so, one of the cubs decided he would like to nurse. Cautiously he approached his mother from behind and timidly thrust his nose up between her hind legs. She never looked around or paused in her activity, but her reaction was immediate and violent. She lashed out savagely with one hind foot and sent the cub hurtling down the steep slope. He should have been killed by the force of the blow, but apparently he was tougher than I thought. Picking himself up out of a clump of brush where he had finally stopped rolling, he made his way slowly back up the hill and crawled into one of the excavations she had abandoned. He crouched in the hole pouting for a long time, head hanging, the picture of abject misery.

The other cub decided to call a recess too, and sat resting in another hole out of the heat. In contrast to the first one, he sat there bright and perky as a little sparrow.

After a while they both came out and resumed their play. It was a relief to see that the cub hadn't suffered any damage from mother's stern rebuke, and after they had rolled over once or twice it was impossible to tell which was which.

Once as they wrestled below the old sow, she turned a boulder twice the size of a soccer ball loose down the hill. The bounding boulder missed the cubs by mere inches, but neither the sow nor the cubs paid it any mind.

After nearly two hours they all made their way down another hundred yards to a little green meadow with a small rill trickling through it. There were a few small potholes filled with water beside the rill. Each cub took possession of one and sat in the cold water with the soles of its little hind feet peeking up over the edge. Mother took a long, satisfying drink, lapping the water like a dog. I was hoping to see the little ones nurse, and indeed it was surprising that they hadn't done so by now. Apparently the sow wasn't in the mood, or perhaps because of her age she didn't have sufficient milk. Neither of the cubs was going to risk another reprimand.

Since I still had many miles to cover, I decided to move on. It would be necessary to return by the same route and it seemed a good idea to let my presence be known now rather than risk a later encounter when conditions might not be so favorable. Thinking to test the hearing ability of the bears, I cleared my throat. They were nearly two hundred yards from me then, but that old sow wheeled around toward me with her ears laid back. I doubt that she saw me, but that little "huff" had been an alien sound. She wheeled again toward the cubs, giving a gruff command, and herded them at a dead run down over the brink of the valley. In a few minutes I saw them climb the opposite side, still going as fast as the little ones could manage.

This episode has to be the most entertaining I ever

witnessed. The savage potential of the old sow in contrast to the complete innocence of the vulnerable cubs was powerfully displayed. She had seemed absolutely indifferent to the cubs, but when danger threatened there was no doubt but that she would have unhesitatingly laid down her life for their protection.

A painter or photographer takes pains to compose a picture, but occasionally we happen upon a natural scene inadvertently or accidentally composed. Such a scene occurred once when I was guiding a hunter in the Wild Horse country.

On this particular morning we had made the long climb from our camp at Wild Horse summit up to timberline and a little beyond. We approached a saddle between two peaks and cautiously moved forward to scan the basin below. The peak to our left was nearly vertical on the east face, dropping abruptly five hundred feet or more to the talus below.

The early morning sun was bright on the rock face. As we moved slowly forward we saw a monstrous billy goat perched on a small pinnacle that jutted out of the otherwise sheer cliff. He was close by us, a little above, and in his new winter coat he set off the scene beautifully. Behind him the cobalt sky was dotted with a few fluffy clouds, matching the white of his pelage; the grey jagged rock of his precarious perch dropped vertically to the talus; below the talus lay a sunbathed green meadow encircling an emerald lake. Below us and sweeping wide to the right, the basin was clothed in short yellowing grasses. Scattered here and there on the grassy slope were clumps of dark, wiry shin-tangle, appearing as though they had been laid out by a professional landscaper. Foliage of the deciduous shrubs added splashes of vivid color here and there. Beyond, the dark spruce forest plunged sharply down to the valley of Summer Lake, and finally Summer Lake itself sparkled in the far distance.

The goat stood there for a long moment regarding us, not in the least perturbed. It would have been an easy kill and an outstanding trophy, provided the horns didn't break off in his spectacular fall. I waited for the hunter's inevitable reaction, but he never took the rifle from where it was slung on his shoulder.

The composition of that scene defied description, and the experience also had the added, moving element of judgment displayed by the hunter. Finally the goat turned slowly and moved off his pinnacle. From our viewpoint it seemed as though he had stepped off into the void, but of course he had taken some hidden ledge to make his retreat. Neither of us spoke for a long time, and for some reason we avoided mentioning the goat for the rest of the day.

The Last Beaver

❖   ❖   ❖

THE MONTH OF MARCH, 1973, was very cold. The temperature had held steady at well below zero Fahrenheit for more than a week. The Kootenay River was completely frozen over from bank to bank, and nearly a foot of snow covered the ice.

The Columbia River Treaty had been ratified recently by the Canadian and United States governments. One of the projects stemming from it was the construction of the Libby Dam in Montana. The Libby impoundment was to extend many miles up the beautiful Kootenay Valley to the small town of Wardner in British Columbia. Now the dam was all but completed, the reservoir had been cleared, the government of British Columbia had expropriated the lands of the farmers in the valley, and willy-nilly they were to be evicted. Move or drown.

More than the farmers were being evicted. With the cutting and clearing of all the trees and brush, the many forms of wildlife in the basin to be flooded were forced to abandon what had been home to them since time immemorial — all in the name of progress. Civilization on the march.

Our son-in-law, Orlando Towes, was one of a crew of men demolishing the old wooden bridge across the Kootenay at Waldo. One night he told us that an old buck beaver had come down the river on the ice that day during the crew's afternoon coffee break. They could see him coming down from the bend, shuffling along and pausing frequently as though uncertain of the reception he would receive from the men grouped around their fire. They watched him curiously as he approached, since it was most unusual to see a beaver out on the ice in broad daylight, a long, long way from open water.

A few yards above the bridge a large cottonwood had been felled in the clearing operation, and some of the limbs had broken off with its fall. The tree had been hauled away, but the limbs remained on the ice. The beaver made his way to these limbs and, while the men watched, fed on the bark. He was obviously nervous. After a while he took a good-sized limb and left the way he had come, dragging the limb behind him.

Obviously he was starving. It was the middle of March, he must have eaten all the winter's supply of food he had been able to store the previous summer before the chainsaws and bulldozers had cleared everything edible away. With another month to go before spring, he was in a critical situation indeed.

The following day he appeared again at the same time and repeated the procedure, retreating up the river once more with a big limb dragging behind. The third day he came as before. This time Orlando went down to where he was feeding. The beaver grew increasingly nervous as Orlando approached, but he desperately held his ground. Orlando picked up a limb about ten feet long and eased up close until he could reach out and stroke the beaver's back with the end of the stick. The beaver was so thin that Orlando could feel every vertebra on his back. The beaver backed off at the touch, and Orlando, not wanting to drive him off his meal, moved away.

The beaver then returned to his interrupted snack, fed for a while, and, taking another limb in his mouth, waddled back upriver. Orlando was so intrigued with the animal's behavior that he followed at a distance to see where he was going with the limb. When he got to the bend in the river, Orlando was surprised to see another beaver, probably the old buck's mate, waiting on the ice. The old buck dragged the limb up to her and watched her as she fed. She was probably too shy to risk approaching the men, so the old buck had done his best to provide for her.

The story of the beavers' plight bothered me and I resolved to do something to help them, like taking an ax and cutting a poplar down somewhere in the hills back from the cleared ground and hauling it in chunks to where the beavers could find it.

The next day was Saturday, but I had some important business to attend to. Orlando thought the beavers had enough cottonwood branches to do them for another day or two. My business was so important that a month later I couldn't remember what it was. Ha!

Sunday morning Alta and I started out in our old pickup truck, armed with a sharp ax, and drove down to the bridge. We didn't need the ax. Just a few yards above where the beavers had fed we found what was left of him, and the story of what had happened was clearly written in the snow. A small pack of coyotes, probably three or four, had caught him on the open ice, killed him, and devoured him. He hadn't died easily or quickly. The beaver, while not a fighter, is a big, tough animal, and judging by the sign, this one had resisted death for some time.

We walked up the river following the trail he had beaten out. We found the sticks where his mate had fed. We found a small heap of driftwood where they had chewed on a few dry sticks in a vain effort to gain some sustenance. A little farther up we found a logjam with a hole in one side where they had tried to take shelter. It had served as some protection from the coyotes, whose tracks were everywhere, but as a shelter from the elements it was worthless. The lifestyle of beavers is such that they must have a proper lodge if they are to survive through the bitter cold of winter. The webs and tails of this pair had probably already become frozen, and if this were the case, no amount of food would have helped them.

We saw no trace of the mate. No doubt she had shared his fate, but we didn't find the spot.

As we walked along we thought about how the beavers had probably come to their fate. Most likely they had been forced by hunger to abandon their home den, and had moved down the river searching for food. Coyotes had discovered their plight, and the beavers had taken cover in the logjam. Searching when they dared, they had found where the cottonwood had been felled and fed there, returning to the logjam between feedings.

The coyotes had probably harassed them to the point where they no longer dared to make the trip down the ice at night, which would be their natural feeding time. But in daylight, with the men working on the bridge, the coyotes kept back. The beavers, desperate for food, took the chance when the crew were quiet at coffee time. But on Saturday when the men were not at work, their luck had run out.

As we know, tragedies like this are all a part of nature. But this was not a part of the natural state. Man, with his insatiable desire to change the face of the earth to suit his idea of Utopia, had wrought the changes that spelled doom to these beavers. And the beavers were not the only ones to suffer. What of all the other wildlife that shared similar fates in that part of the valley? What of the people, the farmers who had slaved for generations to establish what they had believed to be security and a way of life? Of course the farmers were paid for their property, but whether they were paid a fair price is another question. What amount is fair for their homes, lands, the way of life they loved?

Those two beavers may well have been the last of the millions who had made their home in that part of the world for untold centuries. I've often reflected sadly on the irony of this event: our national animal, and we couldn't even take time to haul them a few chunks of poplar.

The latest news I have heard is that Lake Koocanusa is now acting as a settling pond, trapping the nutrients that normally find their way to Kootenay Lake. Because of that, Kootenay Lake is dying. If this is true, and let us hope fervently that it is not, in a few years' time the fabulous rainbow trout of that lake will be gone along with the beavers. What price Koocanusa?

KOOtenay-CANada-USA. Someone took the name of the valley where the Libby dam was being built, added the names of two great and proud nations, and named the new lake Koocanusa, so the whole world would know what a wonder these two nations together had wrought.

Rear View

❖ ❖ ❖

To BRING YOU UP TO DATE on my marriage with Alta, after forty-nine years together we have produced and reared four children, and she is still cooking my meals, washing my clothes, and warming my bed.

It was not until our children were grown and gone that Alta had the time to indulge in some activities she had always yearned to do. When she was in her fifties she took up figure skating. A couple of years later she learned to swim. The year she was sixty she took up cross-country skiing and prevailed on me to do the same. She came from pioneer stock: she is a descendant of the Boone family of Kentucky fame, and the Alta Goodwin who is the central character in Ben East's book, *Silence of the North*, is my Alta's aunt and namesake. It naturally follows that she is right at home in the Great Outdoors. Now we spend much time in the hills and on the streams and lakes together.

We expect to have many good years ahead of us. We both come from long-lived families. My father's father lived to be ninety-eight. My mother's mother died at ninety-four. My mother went on well into her seventies.

Alta's mother is still thin and frail at the age of eight-three, after having borne twelve children. She called us up at eleven-thirty last New Year's Eve to tell us that she was going to a party. Incidentally, at last count she had forty-eight grandchildren and sixty-four great-grandchildren, and by now there must be more of the latter since there were some en route at the time of the count.

Her father (Alta's grandfather) died at ninety-four when he was run over by a truck.

I've been very fortunate to have lived nearly all my life in the great East Kootenay Valley. Not only is it one of the most picturesque spots on earth, but during my lifetime it has been home to a tremendous concentration of wild animals, probably the greatest North America will ever see. These animals have served to vitalize the already beautiful area, and have added immeasurably to the pleasures inherent in the Great Outdoors.

In unbelievable numbers the animals have included bighorn sheep, mountain goats, mule and white-tailed deer; black, brown, and grizzly bears; elk, moose, caribou; predators such as the cougar, coyote, wolverine, lynx, and bobcat; and a host of birds and other animals. Many of us can recall a time when it was possible to drive out to the Bull River country on a spring evening and count several species of wild animals numbering in the hundreds beside the road. Sadly, now many of these species are in decline, victims of the burgeoning human population.

I've lived amidst plenty and have pursued an avocation that led me to spend much time in the wilderness, so I have had many interesting adventures. I have been witness to dramas of the wild that are forever taking place — many that the average person never sees.

If I could influence any of our young hunters I would like to suggest that they go out and hunt at every opportunity, but they shouldn't feel cheated if they don't fill all their tags. The killing of game is of course an inherent part of hunting, but it should not be considered the most important part.

There's a lot more out there than is set forth in the hunting regulations.

INDEX

All places and organizations are in British Columbia unless stated otherwise.

ABOUT THE AUTHOR

ERNEST F. "FEE" HELLMEN grew up around Cranbrook on the edge of the lower Canadian Rockies. Born in 1918 in a two-room log cabin near Wardner, British Columbia, he was the son of a logger and his family lived off the land.

After a life of outdoor adventures and big-game guiding, at age 64 Hellmen began a writing career, contributing a weekly outdoor column to the Cranbrook *Kootenay Advertiser*. Many of those newspaper stories were rewritten and included in this book, marking the culmination of Hellmen's lifetime love affair with the jagged and beautiful Canadian Rocky Mountain Range.

Fee Hellmen has been a member of the Outdoor Writers of Canada. Now retired, he lives in Cranbrook, and still roams the hills with his wife, Alta, and their grown children.